Invest Yourself is a sincere, concise, passionate challenge for believers on biblical authority and principles, this resource lovingly provides fulfilling the call and privilege of Christ-centered mentorship.

—Bryan Osborne
Author and Speaker for Answers in Genesis

There are so many voices that limit our potential. Stephanie calls out to us to be who we could be in the lives of other people. She reminds us that true success is truly being significant in other people's lives. She gives us inspirational and practical insight to impact people's lives. I'm so grateful for her and this book!

—Naeem Fazal
Author, Artist and Founding Pastor of Mosaic Church

For those who aspire to fulfill the Great Commission through deep and enduring relationships, but who feel they lack the experience and confidence needed to engage, Stephanie Ziebarth has created a full-on manual that leaves no question unanswered. In twelve easy-to-read chapters, she draws on her own journey to address the why, who, when, where and how of spiritual mentoring. The four-part appendix that follows is rich with resources. If you want to master meaningful one-to-one ministry, this toolkit will provide the guidance and motivation you need.

—John Ashmen
President, Citygate Network

If you desire to intentionally mentor others, helping them walk with God and grow to the point in their spiritual maturity where they can do the same for others, then this book is for you. Stephanie presents both the conceptual anchors for mentoring others, rooting these concepts in the Bible, and many practical helps to put these principles into action. You'll find this book both inspiring and easy to apply as you seek to change the world one person at a time!

—Tom Yeakley
Staff Equipper, The Navigators

Stephanie Ziebarth has provided everything you need to start your mentoring journey. *Invest Yourself* demystifies the sometimes threatening and challenging call to engage others and to help them grow spiritually. The practical information and the inspiring stories outline all you need to fulfill God's commission to make disciples.

—Dan Bolin
Director of Christian Camping International (Retired)

Invest Yourself: A Guidebook for Spiritual Mentoring by Stephanie Ziebarth is a treasure waiting to be discovered. This thought-provoking literary work has transformed our way of thinking regarding spiritual mentorship. Practical steps have been integrated with the Holy Scriptures to provide information and inspiration to assist the reader in embracing different approaches to mentorship. It is a must-read.

—Bishop Ronald and Lady LaShawn Demery
Christ Way Cathedral

Invest Yourself is a very helpful and practical support for those who are serious about mentoring or discipling others. This book takes the mystery out of what to do as we mentor someone and gives detailed, realistic advice on what to share and how to do it! A must-have for anyone who desires to help someone grow in their walk with Jesus!

—Dana Yeakley
Author and Staff with The Navigators

My wife and I have known Stephanie and her husband Aaron for many years. Their love for God and the gifts given by Him have been used to bless many people. We have seen them share these truths in their own sphere and in other countries as well. Stephanie's heart for spiritual mentoring has been poured out through these pages. Her years of caring for the souls of others and intentional collection of excellent resources will be a tremendous insight in assisting individuals to understand the dynamics behind mentoring. May the Lord use this guidebook in a mighty way to inspire you, the reader, to "invest yourself" to further the Kingdom of God and bring glory to our Lord and Savior Jesus the Christ.

—Tom Harmon
Itinerant Preacher, Author and Ministry Leader

This guidebook addresses the exponential power of "the one and the one more." As believers, we are called by our Savior to play a role in the Great Commission. If your thoughts are anywhere along the lines of "I don't have time…" or "My life isn't perfect enough…" or "I feel called, but I don't even know where to start…", then this guidebook is for you! Allow this book to walk you through the practical steps of your mentoring journey "with one" so the multiplication of "the one more" can unfold and fulfill the promises of heaven.

—Tyree Sterling
Pastor, Speaker and Ministry Coach

Having been involved in a college-age discipleship program for more than thirty years, I believe Stephanie Ziebarth has written a tremendous and succinct resource not only for veteran mentors, but also for those just getting started. Her pragmatic approach gives feet to Christ's command to all believers in the Great Commission. Stephanie highlights the importance of a clear emphasis on the use of God's Word, balanced with an intentional relational component. Her heart for mentoring others is evident throughout the book. *Invest Yourself* is a rich, how-to book for life-on-life ministry, and it is a resource I'll both use and recommend.

—Matt Cox
Executive Director of Miracle Mountain Ranch
Home of the School of Discipleship

The apostle Paul exhorted the church to "[redeem] the time, because the days are evil" (Ephesians 5:16 NKJV). Paul's observation to get back what we have lost over time certainly applies to the charge the church received to mentor young men and women and thus make disciples. We have lost it over time. *Invest Yourself* is a timely book my ministers and youth pastors will find to be an "essential" tool in our endeavors to reach this generation. Stephanie's candid transparency makes this book endearing, and her expository delivery gives our church a practical approach to mentoring this generation.

—Rev. Dr. Clenard H. Childress, Jr.
Senior Pastor of New Calvary Baptist Church, Newark, NJ

Stephanie challenges us to make disciples in every moment of our lives, pursuing honesty and simplicity in sharing experiences and the Word of God. This book is not just what to do; this book also brings the great tools of "how to do."

—Christian Aguilar
Pastor of Vida Life Church
Executive Director of Fruitbelt Farmworker Christian Ministry

Invest Yourself is at once an impactful and practical guide on how to share the gospel of Jesus Christ. Stephanie weaves a tight and approachable narrative on how you can mentor others to fulfill the Great Commission together by sharing stories from her mentors and her experiences. Most of all, Stephanie relies on God and

His powerful Word to deliver a timeless approach in a new way that brings God glory and helps all who endeavor to invest in others. Stephanie's message is clear: God's returns are limitless!

—Travis L. Zimmerman
Pastor and Founder of A Faithful Dad Ministry

Invest Yourself: A Guidebook for Spiritual Mentoring by Stephanie Ziebarth is the most complete and detailed outline for effective spiritual counseling I have ever read. Over the past fifty-two years the Lord has blessed me to provide values clarification to the incarcerated, bereavement counseling to former prisoners who have lost a loved one, and spiritual mentoring to parolees and those who are struggling with various habits, hangups and pains. However, I have never encountered such a powerful and organized tool as *Invest Yourself*. It not only enlightened me on why my mentoring may not have been as effective as it could have been, but also is an outline itself on how to do better. If your calling is spiritual mentoring, or if you have a desire to do so effectively, this book is a must companion and guide. I thank God for using Stephanie to provide this needed gem to the world. If you are serious about giving God your best in this line of work, get this book and make it one of your closest companions.

—Dr. James Jenkins, M. Ministry, D. Divinity
Pastor of The Compassion of Christ Church DC Inc.

Invest Yourself provides fantastic step-by-step instructions for mentoring with excellence. Stephanie's heart for disciple-making shines through as she casts vision and provides tools that new mentors need to begin their journey. Practical, purposeful and relevant, this manual delivers much-needed guidance for anyone willing to invest in the lives of others.

—Nancy Morton, MSW, LCSW

Stephanie is the real deal. She cares deeply about seeing people grow in their walk with Jesus, and the experiences and ideas she shares here are helpful and straightforward. This is a valuable guidebook full of practical advice for anyone interested in one-on-one mentoring and encouraging people spiritually.

—Benjamin Raber
Executive Director of NETWork Ministries

Stephanie is an incredible example of what it means to invest in the next generation of faith-based leaders. Within this book, you will find a simple but profound pathway for developing disciples through a personal, mentoring process. Stephanie takes the valued principle of personal mentorship and provides a roadmap on getting started. If you are in a position to mentor youth or train mentors of youth, this book will help you increase your effectiveness. Thank you, Stephanie, for your wisdom and insight. Looking forward to implementing this in my own mentoring relationships.

—Chad Chute
Executive Pastor, Grand Point Church, Chambersburg, PA

INVEST
YOURSELF

A Guidebook for
Spiritual Mentoring

STEPHANIE ZIEBARTH

Paperback ISBN 978-1-945169-74-8
eBook ISBN 978-1-945169-75-5

Mercy & Moxie
An Imprint of
Orison Publishers, Inc.
PO Box 188, Grantham, PA 17027
www.OrisonPublishers.com

Permission to reprint "Walking by Faith with the Promises of God" by Tom Yeakley granted by Tom Yeakley.

Author photo by Andrea Ziebarth.

Scripture quotations marked (NIV) are taken from The Holy Bible, New International Version® NIV®, copyright © 1973, 1978, 1984, 2011 by Biblica, Inc.™ Used by permission. All rights reserved worldwide.

Scripture quotations marked (NKJV) are taken from the New King James Version®, copyright © 1982 by Thomas Nelson. Used by permission. All rights reserved.

Scripture quotations marked (NLT) are taken from the Holy Bible, New Living Translation, copyright ©1996, 2004, 2015 by Tyndale House Foundation. Used by permission of Tyndale House Publishers, a Division of Tyndale House Ministries, Carol Stream, Illinois 60188. All rights reserved.

Scripture quotations marked (WEB) are taken from the World English Bible. Public domain.

CONTENTS

FOREWORD

In an age of ever-increasing specialization, it's nice to learn that you can do something that is simple and profound without an advanced degree. You can mentor another person and change the trajectory of lives eternally. Not only is this a biblical model for ministry, but it also lies within the reach of normal people. No special licensure or advanced training is required. A person who wants to reach and raise up disciples in our generation just needs to step up.

So, why are most people stepping back? Why aren't more mentors coming onboard to reach and raise up a generation of young disciples? I don't propose to have all the answers, but I'll make a couple of observations after twenty-five years of ministry to college students: Most of us don't take initiative because *we don't know where to start*…or what to do after we start. Our age of specialization brings with it expectations of precision and expertise. If we do not know where to begin, how to proceed or what might result from our efforts, we simply don't begin at all. Stephanie Ziebarth cannot tell you *what will result from your efforts*, but she can help you know *where to begin* and *how to proceed* in a mentoring relationship. The book you are about to read is a book of practical vision. Most of us need a model if we're going to move ahead in a disciple-making direction. *Invest Yourself* will provide just such a model.

There's another factor at play that keeps many of us from mentoring others: we're afraid of people. That's not to say we're afraid to give a speech (I'm not) or engage in a street fight (I am). Most of us are simply afraid of failing, so we avoid environments of uncertainty. We limit ourselves to processes and programs with largely predictable outcomes, and *people are not predictable*. Mentoring people is not safe in that way. We don't know whether people will be receptive to our initial overtures. We don't know whether they will ask us hard questions. We don't know whether they will tell us the truth when we ask them hard questions. There's so much we don't know *because people are unpredictable*. And we are afraid of failure. Developing relationships exposes us to risks we'd rather avoid. So, we default to program-centered ministries: we secure a location, adopt a curriculum and invite people to come to a meeting. Meetings are not bad in and of themselves, of course, but inviting people to meetings and mentoring people are not the same thing. Mentoring means developing deepening relationships with others. *Invest Yourself* will give you the courage to try.

If you've glanced at the contents of this book, you probably see that there's more to be done than to *talk about* the importance of mentoring. It's time to take steps of action. Reflecting on the way that Paul modeled and mentored young believers, Craig Blomberg and Darlene Seal say, "We do not need new discipleship programs, just mature and honest mentors whom we can watch to understand how believers should live…."[1] Thankfully, Stephanie Ziebarth has written a concise book that will provide you with the inspiration and guidance you need to do just that. Mentoring another person is the everyday work of ordinary believers. You can do this!

Norman and Kristy Hubbard
Serving with The Navigators
The University of Minnesota
Minneapolis College

PREFACE

Welcome to an opportunity to change a life!

And not just one life. When you serve as a spiritual mentor, God gives you the opportunity to change not only the life of the person you are mentoring, but also your own life as well as the lives of countless others whose paths intersect with yours and your mentee's—now and in the future.

It may seem like a simple thing to sit down with another Christ-follower and talk about life and Jesus, but there is so much more to it. Approach this mentoring adventure with an open heart and a faith "as a mustard seed" that can move mountains (Matthew 17:20 NIV). Call to God and ask Him to show you "great and mighty things" that you "do not know" (Jeremiah 33:3 NKJV). I believe you will see God work powerfully—and you will be so grateful He chose you to impact others for His glory.

As we get started with this mentoring guide, I should mention that all names have been changed within this book, with the exception of that of my mentor, Debby Maschhoff.

It also might help to clarify that when I refer to "spiritual mentoring" throughout this book, I am referring to influencing, guiding and directing someone's spiritual journey. When Debby and I met together during my college years, we called it discipleship, and it was a very intentional process. I find the term "mentoring" to be more easily understood and more flexible than "discipleship," so that is why I prefer that term. However, the spiritual mentoring process we will explore within this guidebook will still be very intentional and still accomplish what Jesus asked of us when He said, "Go therefore and make disciples…" (Matthew 28:18 NKJV).

Please join me as God reveals the power of mentoring through this guidebook.

Chapter One
THE IMPACT OF MENTORSHIP

I grew up in a home where I dealt with drama on a regular basis. In spite of the drama, I sensed the Lord's presence at a young age. With alcoholism in the family, I dealt with things that scar even an adult. Thankfully, my mother had an awareness of a heavenly Father. In the midst of her suffering, she passed that awareness on to her children.

My parents separated, then divorced. Fortunately, my mother and soon-to-be-stepfather found a gospel-teaching church shortly after beginning their relationship. Thus, while in elementary school, I learned about my own sin, my need for a Savior, and the fact that Jesus is that Savior. I enthusiastically entrusted my young heart to Jesus.

As is common with the human race, more drama lay ahead as my wounded parents attempted to make a new life with their blended family. I am thankful that during that time I sensed my heavenly Father's presence. He always was drawing me to Him, and one place where He did that was at camp.

I first attended Camp Shamineau in Motley, Minnesota, as an elementary school student. Shamineau (pronounced SHA-min-ah) was a safe, healthy and fun place where I could be myself and learn about Jesus. God later used my years serving on the camp's high school staff to impress upon me the importance of serving Jesus with all my heart and of entrusting Him with every single aspect of my life. Under the guidance of a good staff leader at Shamineau (whom I would later marry), I began spending time daily with the Lord in His Word and in prayer.

By God's grace, I found I was a natural leader—a trait that served me well when I began my journalism degree at the University of Minnesota. A camp acquaintance motivated me to join The Navigators (a Christian ministry focused on discipleship) on campus. I got involved with the small band of Christian students. Our numbers grew quickly, mainly through friends beginning relationships with Jesus after hearing the gospel message.

Soon our group included several young women who were new in their Christian faith, and our group was led solely by two young men. These young men approached me and asked if I would step up to help lead these young women. Although intimidated, since I had just started college and joined the group, I agreed. After I committed to helping lead, one of the students in the group approached me with a pleasant bonus. He said, "My parents are actually on staff with The Navigators. My mom said she'd start meeting with you. She told me, 'I don't have time to get too involved with this, but give me one student. I have time for one.' I told her, 'That's easy: Steph.'" Receiving mentoring from a seasoned ministry leader would help me better lead those in our college group.

Little did I know that what I initially considered a "pleasant bonus" would become a life-changing relationship with a mentor.

The first time I met with Debby Maschhoff, I was ready. We sat across from each other in the student union building, and I told her my unedited life story. I was thrilled to have personal access to a godly woman who was willing to answer my questions and help me grow in my relationship with Jesus. This seasoned mentor already had discipled dozens of women before me, and now I had the opportunity to grow under her guidance. I ate up everything she had to say to me. Toward the end of our time together that day, she handed me a little book called *Lessons on Assurance* by The Navigators to read and asked me to memorize 1 John 5:11-12 for our next meeting. I previously had memorized Scripture only for youthful church competitions, but I was so eager to grow that I did exactly as she asked.

At the time, neither Debby nor I knew what God had in store for us. However, we both wanted to please Him and to make the most of this relationship. He blessed us by providing us with four incredibly fruitful years of discipleship. I was receptive to what Debby had to teach me, and she was faithful to continually invest in me.

Our emphasis was certainly on my relationship with Jesus, but she also provided mentoring in almost every area of my life. Debby recognized the talent and potential hidden beneath the insecurities I nursed as a young college student. She helped to excavate those gifts—and along the way helped me to grow in confidence, leadership, love, faith and a joyful outlook.

This marvelous woman helped me to develop the very habits you want to nurture in your mentees: making God's Word their primary text for life, actively seeking God through prayer, sharing Jesus with others, having a positive impact on their communities, doing all things for the glory of God, as well as other good life principles.

I can look back at that time and say that Debby's fingerprints are all over my life. She has influenced me as a person, a Christian, a wife, a mother, a friend, a neighbor, a leader and a mentor to others.

All along, her plan was that I would pass on what she was giving to me. Disappointingly, I got off to a slow start; my first attempts at mentoring lacked chemistry or the needed commitment level. Eventually, during my senior year in college, I began meeting with a young woman named Missy. We got along wonderfully, and Missy was eager to grow. Today, Missy serves as a missionary in a country that requires "creativity" in bringing the gospel message.[1]

After Missy came a long line of women whom I have had the opportunity to mentor. Debby has continued mentoring others as well. What began as me sitting across the table from Debby in the University of Minnesota student union building has now become a network of generations of women influenced by both of us (as well as those who earlier invested in Debby). The connections continue to spread, and *you* are now a part of that network.

It never ceases to amaze me how God can take flawed human beings like Debby and me and use us to influence the world for Jesus Christ! You are no different. Are you ready for Him to do the same with you?

Chapter Two

MENTORING BASICS 101

Mentoring is a commitment. At its simplest level, when you agree to mentor someone, you are making a serious investment. It requires discipline and time. Not only will you need time to actually get together, but mentoring also requires planning for your meetings, touching base during your times apart, and praying faithfully for your mentee. You are in charge of setting the direction of the mentoring relationship, which is a great responsibility (see James 3:1).

The most important aspect of mentoring, perhaps, is exhibiting your own personal, growing relationship with Jesus Christ. Your life will set an example for your mentee, and you can be sure that he or she will be watching closely. Many years ago, a mentee who had moved away to attend seminary brought her fiancé to meet me. I was shocked when she shared with him and me that one of the biggest lessons she learned from me had to do with parenting. We had never even addressed parenting, but we did meet inside my home with my small children underfoot. She had been watching much more closely than I had realized.

The moment you realize how much influence you have is usually the time when you start to feel intimidated. Let me reassure you: you just need to be further along in the journey of following Jesus than your mentee. You will never be perfect, and neither will your mentee. If you humbly seek the Lord and prayerfully ask Him to work through you, you will be able to share with others what He has taught you.

One of the most powerful ways you can help your mentee is by serving as his or her prayer warrior. Many years ago, a lovely young woman in the mentoring program I coordinate asked a woman from her church to be her mentor. The potential mentor called me, distraught and unsure. We talked and prayed through the concerns she shared, and the two women ultimately met for five years of mentoring. Sometime during year two, the mentor shared the following with me:

> I was especially concerned about serving as Ellen's mentor because my own teen daughter had recently gotten pregnant outside of marriage. I thought, *How can I possibly invest in Ellen when I have failed my own daughter?* Then I realized that these young women are fighting against cultural and spiritual influences that can easily overpower them, which my own family had experienced in a bittersweet way! I knew then and there that I could be Ellen's prayer warrior. Perhaps more than other potential mentors, I knew how much prayer Ellen would need, and I would absolutely commit to intentionally praying for her.

A mentoring relationship also needs a goal, a purpose. You will develop a vision for how your mentee might grow within the timeframe you two have set for the mentoring period (which may be either a defined period of time or an indefinite period). Since a summer camp is part of the ministry where I serve, I often mentor a summer staff member. We generally meet weekly for about ten weeks. Very early on, I ask God and the mentee for guidance on an area where growth is needed. I assess (with her help, as I mentor young women) where my mentee is at in that area, where she would like to be, and the most likely way we can get there during our times together. I draft a plan for how we will use our time at each meeting, and we move forward with the plan, adapting it as we go. At the end of the summer, I ask the mentee to evaluate her own growth.

Your mentoring relationship will affect both you and your mentee in eternal ways. It also will build up your local body of believers as you and your mentee set an example for others—an example that will catch on with your fellow Christians. Your mentee holds the potential to shape the future of the local church as well as the global Body of Christ. Without a doubt, as a mentor, what you pass on to your mentee will be passed on to many others in the future.

We will examine these topics more deeply as you progress through this guidebook. My prayer is that you and your mentee will walk alongside one another through life, encouraging, challenging and strengthening each other; providing accountability for one another; and loving each other as Christ calls us to love one another (see John 13:34-35). As you do, you will find yourself becoming an effective spiritual coach, director, disciple-maker and, of course, mentor—one whose relationships have eternal value.

Let me lay out the potential impact for you. Debby mentored me, and I passed that on to Missy. Missy spent decades serving in a creative access country,[1] sharing the gospel and training believers to share Jesus in even further contexts. Some of those women went into still more dangerous countries where they risked their lives to bring the hope of Christ to those who did not know God. Ponder that. Debby, Missy and I have spiritual children and grandchildren around the globe. The same can happen for you. You may attend the same church your entire life, but you can affect the future and impact the world by deliberately pouring your life and lessons into another person.

Ready to get started? Answer the following questions, thinking carefully about your responses.

1. What is required of you as you begin a mentoring relationship? Are you mentally and emotionally prepared for this commitment?

2. Why is it important for your own walk with the Lord Jesus to be personally strong as a mentor?

3. What are some possible goals for a mentor/mentee relationship? Brainstorm some ideas here.

Chapter Three
SPIRITUAL MULTIPLICATION

I did not understand spiritual multiplication before meeting Debby. She taught the concept to me through Scripture and through what she was doing in my life. To understand the awesome privilege of mentoring, it will be helpful to have a firm grasp on the idea of spiritual multiplication. After all, we've got a world of almost eight billion people to reach with the hope offered through Jesus Christ. Spiritual multiplication is the plan God laid out for us to accomplish this task.

When I conduct a training session for mentors, I usually draw x's on a whiteboard to represent each person in the room. On the opposite side of the whiteboard, I write the number eight billion, representing the current world population. I then pose the question, "How many people have you guided into a personal relationship with Jesus Christ in the past year?" After a few moments (or minutes) of silence, someone may hesitantly raise a hand and say, "I think one." Someone else might think to mention a daughter or son. We might manage to put up to five x's on the board next to our original x's to show how quickly we're sharing the gospel with those who do not know Jesus.

This can be a somber moment. All of us sitting in the room have the key to eternal life. We all know in our hearts how important it is to spread this knowledge, but we often fall short in doing so.

1. Open your Bible to 2 Timothy 2:2. Read the verse and then list all the people mentioned within it, as well as how they are connected.

This verse is not a prominent, oft-memorized verse, and you may not fully understand what I am getting at with my question. So, let me lay it out.

Paul is speaking to Timothy. Paul has been teaching him (in the presence of many witnesses, who also are benefiting from this instruction). Paul wants Timothy to take what Paul has given him and intentionally pass it on to other people whom Timothy knows will be teachable and reliable—people who will continue to pass on the truth that they have received. In this way, Paul and Timothy both are effectively transmitting the life-changing, eternity-determining message of how we can have peace with God through Christ.

This provides us with a more encouraging "x scenario":

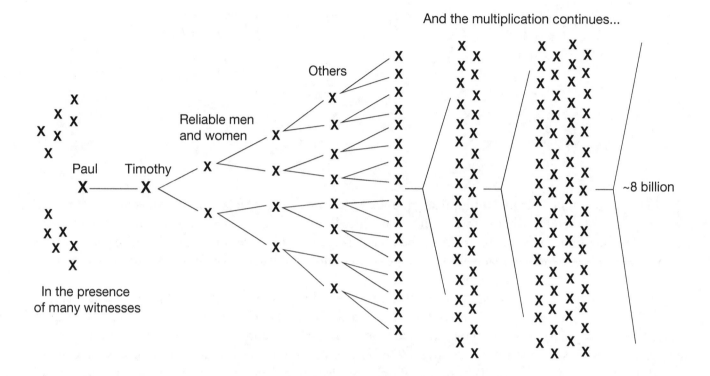

This is spiritual multiplication: we take what God has given us, starting with the gospel, and pass it on to others.

When someone joins God's family, he or she is spiritually like an infant. Actual babies cannot raise themselves. They are completely dependent on others to meet their basic needs. Spiritual babies do not do much better. They flounder along in the faith, perhaps landing in a decent church, but possibly remaining spiritually stagnant. Rather than leaving these spiritual infants to raise themselves, we should nurture and instruct them, giving them tools that will help them grow. When they thrive and grow as spiritually healthy beings, they will be able to pass on their wisdom and experience to others. This is evangelism partnered with discipleship—what we are referring to as mentoring—rather than evangelism on its own. It is much more effective because it leads to exponential growth rather than mathematical growth. To put it another way, evangelism with discipleship might seem slower at first because it's done one-on-one or in small groups, but the results are longer-lasting, and thus more people are impacted in the long term.

Of course, this raises a natural question: if this idea is so good, why haven't we reached the global population yet? I believe we haven't because we as individuals don't tend to fully appreciate both sides of this double-edged sword of evangelism and discipleship. We tend to have a heart and aptitude for one or the other. So we either share the gospel and leave our potential mentees to figure out growth and spiritual multiplication on their own, or we want to mentor teachable people but, because we enjoy each other's company so much, we forget to go out into the world to spread the gospel among the hopeless souls around us.

Sadly, some Christians practice neither evangelism nor discipleship. However, we need to practice both. Yes, we may have a natural affinity for one over the other, but God calls us to both.

2. Besides Paul and Timothy, who are some other examples in Scripture of someone more mature investing in someone who wants to grow?

Pairs like Elijah and Elisha, Moses and Joshua, and Barnabas and Paul are often the first to come to mind. But also consider pairs like Eli and Samuel in 1 Samuel 3–4 as well as Naomi and Ruth. Eli and Naomi both had weaknesses that are clear in Scripture, yet God used them to mentor those entrusted to their care. For example, Naomi surely modeled something powerful about the God of Israel because Ruth left her family, country, gods and all else familiar in order to follow Naomi and her God on a perilous journey and into a difficult life. Mentors like Eli and Naomi remind us that God can use us even when we feel unusable.

As you run across these relationships in your Bible reading, learn from their example and apply those lesson to your own mentoring relationships.

Did you include Jesus when you listed scriptural examples of mentoring relationships? Jesus is the prime example for mentoring. Discipleship was the crux of His three-year, history-shaping, public ministry. He primarily invested in twelve ordinary men. He entrusted the key to eternal life to them, equipping and challenging them to share it across the world as they knew it.

3. Read some of Jesus's final words to His disciples in Matthew 28:18-20, which is known as the Great Commission. (Final words are worth serious consideration.) What does Jesus ask of His followers? (Please don't miss that the commission actually includes more than just sharing the gospel!)

4. Some Bible teachers, such as Kenny Burchard, clarify that "go" is closer to "as you are going" in the Greek.[1] What new light does this information shed on your understanding of the Great Commission in Matthew 28?

We are to be passing on God's message wherever we are, whatever we are doing, all along the way. We can pass it on to our mentees while we work on a project together, as we drive, while we're sitting in a restaurant, as we open God's Word together—always. We can model it, and not just to our mentees. We also should model for and share with our server, stylist, accountant, aquatics instructor, and every other person with whom we interact "as we are going."

5. Another of Jesus's final earthly appearances is recorded in John 21:15-17. What does Jesus ask Peter here?

6. How many times does He ask this?

7. What does it usually mean if something is repeated multiple times, for example, during a lecture?

8. What does Jesus say to Peter each time Peter insists that he loves Jesus?

Jesus makes clear a direct connection between our love for Him and our nurturing of His flock. He wants us to show *Him* our love by caring for our brothers and sisters in Christ. We are loving Christ when we love and invest in our mentee (see 2 Corinthians 9:12).

We also can make a real difference in the world around us as we model for our mentees a faith that is outward as well as inward. Mark Moore, a teaching pastor at Christ's Church of the Valley in Peoria, Arizona, makes the point that the "greatest commandments" (found in Matthew 22:36-40) are tied to the Great Commission.[2] When we love our neighbors, we model for our mentees how to have an outward focus.

Let us love one another as we seek to reach the world.

Chapter Four
THREE ASPECTS OF APPROACH

Mentoring is fairly popular right now. People seem to recognize the value in the personalized instruction provided through mentoring relationships. In fact, my neighbor works in a high-security prison, where the staff incorporate mentoring into the training of new guards. While we don't often think of something as warm and fuzzy as mentoring in a harsh prison environment, my neighbor would quickly convince you of what is at stake.

When my neighbor enters a certain area of the prison, he has to "suit up" in protective gear from head to toe. This is not protective apparel in the sense of combat gear; rather, it shields the guards from whatever horrible things the prisoners may throw at them. Some prisoners make use of whatever resources they have to degrade those who guard them, including throwing their own feces. These prison workers need to protect their dignity and health upon entering these areas. Not only that, but their safety is at stake. Even through bars, a person can be killed by someone who is determined enough to do so.

Prison mentors pass on to trainees the seriousness of their tasks and the utmost care they need to take in performing them. One misstep can have dire consequences.

Fortunately, our mentoring relationships have a much more pleasant nature. We have the joy of getting to know a brother or sister in Christ who wants to grow. However, the implications are even more serious because we are focusing on issues of eternity and seeking to use these relationships to reach the world for Christ.

We may find our mentee a little guarded or unsure at first. This is natural and should not deter us. Any relationship needs time, effort, established trust and honest communication to move forward. Once trust and communication are proven, we have the privilege of helping these mentees focus on Christ as the center of their lives.

How we gain trust and progress will look different within each mentoring relationship. All mentors and mentees have different personalities. I have seen all manner of combinations within the mentoring program I currently coordinate through Joy El Generation,[1] and that is a beautiful thing.

Later we will expand on how and where you might start with your mentee; however, as a rule of guidance, here are three major approaches to consider for your own approach to any mentoring relationship.

Be Structural (*Have a plan*)
Consider writing down a mission statement for this relationship, even though you may need to revise it along the way. Set goals. Plan for how each time together can move you toward your goals. Above all, be sure your purpose is focused on Jesus and enveloped in prayer.

My mentor, Debby, trained me to focus on these key areas in mentoring and equipping people for ministry:

- assurance of salvation (or understanding the gospel)
- God's Word (emphasizing daily time in the Bible)
- Scripture memorization
- prayer
- fellowship
- witnessing
- meditation/application
- faith
- obedience

The idea is to start at the top of that list and work your way down, not moving on to the next topic until evidence is seen that the mentee understands and is growing in that area. One focus I added as essential in mentoring is identity in Christ. I cover that topic early in a mentoring relationship because I have found that most believers do not have a grasp on who they are in Christ, which has a powerful impact on how they live (see Ephesians 2:10).

You can find resources for these topics in Appendix A.

1. If you don't have structure, what might happen within your mentoring relationship?

You don't want to waste the precious time you have with this child of God. You want to make the most of it.

2. Most good things have a flip side. What could happen if you become too structured?

No one likes to be a project. Younger generations are particularly sensitive to this thought. Even while being intentional, you may need to be very casual about your plan—especially at first. You will prove your genuine concern for your mentee through the approaches described in this chapter.

Another reason you do not want to be overly structured is that you need to rely on the Holy Spirit. Sometimes a plan may need to change to meet a need of the moment, but you can still remain focused on the greater purpose.

Be Relational (Meet needs)

We must be attuned to emotional needs. Without this attentiveness, we will not have a truly loving and Christ-like relationship. If a person comes to a one-on-one time with a pressing need, he or she is going to be distracted by that need until it is addressed. Taking the time to address the need is also a prime opportunity to model how we cast our cares upon the Lord, who meets our needs (see 1 Peter 5:7). Once the "felt need" is addressed, we can move on to our planned purpose.

In other words, we should keep our purpose in mind, but we also need to be adaptable. This willingness to adapt promotes dependence on the Holy Spirit and authenticates our concern for our mentee.

3. Looking at the flip side again, what is the potential disadvantage of focusing too much on meeting emotional needs?

During my college years of meeting with Debby, my friends quickly noticed how much I was growing as a result of this relationship. Scripture was flowing out of my mouth in daily speech, I could provide biblical counsel, and I was praying with more confidence and fervor. Suddenly, my closer friends all wanted mentors. Debby began encouraging her women friends to meet with these eager young Christ-followers.

Haley was one of my college friends seeking a mentor. She began meeting with a woman named Dinorah, who was new to mentoring. Dinorah didn't know Haley well enough to know that Haley's temperament was somewhat emotionally driven at that stage in her life. Each week, Haley would get together with Dinorah, only to pour out her heart about the crisis at hand. Perhaps she had a concern regarding the boy she liked, she was confused about her major, or she was fighting with a friend. Each week, Dinorah set aside her initial plan in order to walk Haley through what seemed significant in that moment.

Haley would stop by my dorm room after her meetings with Dinorah and fill me in on how things went. Having known Haley for many years, I could see what was happening. Sure enough, one day Haley informed me that she was ending things with Dinorah. "We never get anywhere," Haley explained. "It's not a good use of my time."

Although we need to be sensitive to our mentee's emotional needs, we cannot let them trump the overall goal of knowing Christ and making Him known. We need to address the needs of the moment but still return to our goal.

Another grave consideration for this aspect of approach is that we do not want to foster emotional dependence on us as the mentor. Mentoring should feel fulfilling. Having someone need and/or admire us can make us feel important. However, that is only temporarily satisfying. When we have a mentee texting us morning, noon and night, something starts to feel wrong (and exhausting). These relationships are about Jesus (see 1 Corinthians 2:3-5). We are helping our mentees develop their dependency on Christ, not on us.

One-on-one relationships can be the most powerful form of spiritual instruction because they are tailored to the individuals and the circumstances. However, they also can be the most dangerous. We do not want to create any unhealthy dependencies, nor do we want to lead our mentees astray. We need to have a balanced approach, and we need to stay connected to a larger body of believers.

Be Personal *(Get to know each other)*
This is where the friendship element enters. Enjoy each other. Have fun! Exhibit thoughtful gestures. This is important in showing your love, so your mentees know that they are not projects.

4. Read 1 Thessalonians 2:8. What does Paul say he is delighted to share with the Thessalonians?

Note that Paul sandwiches his message in loving language. We were "*delighted* to share with you not only the gospel of God but our lives as well" because "*we loved you so much.*" Also note that they *became* dear to them; it was not instant. However, I do believe Christ offers us His loving nature toward others, which is possible to show early in a relationship.

5. What are some possible disadvantages of focusing on the friendship aspect of our mentoring relationships?

As precious as they are to us, friends are easier to find than mentors. If I asked such a question and had people raise their hands in a group setting, almost everyone would acknowledge having been blessed with multiple meaningful friendships. Hands would not be raised as quickly when asked whether people could think of life-changing mentors in their lives.

Give your mentee this gift of a mentor. Be part of expanding the Kingdom of God in this powerful way.

* * *

Are you intimidated as you consider these three aspects of approach? I often am nervous as I begin a new mentoring relationship. I know myself well enough to be painfully aware of my weaknesses. However, God somehow uses me anyway. Here is a passage I often turn to for encouragement:

> And if you spend yourselves in behalf of the hungry and satisfy the needs of the oppressed, then your light will rise in the darkness, and your night will become like the noonday. The Lord will guide you always; he will satisfy your needs in a sun-scorched land and will strengthen your frame. You will be like a well-watered garden, like a spring whose waters never fail. –Isaiah 58:10-11 (NIV)

God is your Guide, your Satisfaction and your Strength as you seek to invest in His followers. Regardless of your personality and gifting, rely on Him as you invest in this child of God. And remember, be *structural, relational* and *personal.*

Chapter Five

THREE ESSENTIALS FOR EACH ONE-TO-ONE MEETING

Now that you have three things to keep in mind regarding your mentoring approach, here are three essentials to include in each of your times with your mentee.

God's Word

Dirk Van Zuylen, former National Director of Navigators UK, said, "The effectiveness of our disciplemaking will be proportionate to the place God's Word has in our lives."[1]

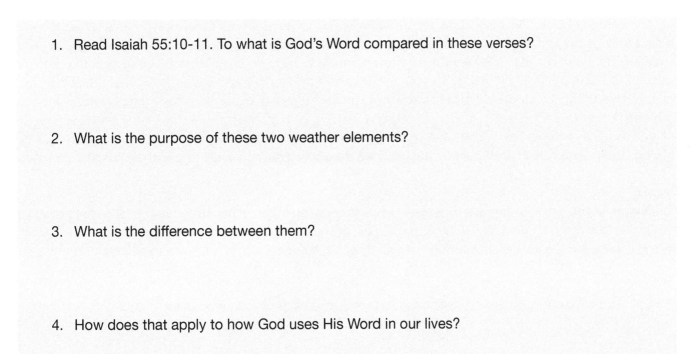

1. Read Isaiah 55:10-11. To what is God's Word compared in these verses?

2. What is the purpose of these two weather elements?

3. What is the difference between them?

4. How does that apply to how God uses His Word in our lives?

If you concluded that God's Word accomplishes its purpose, you are correct! However, sometimes the timing of this accomplishment may be a little different than what we are expecting. Snow and rain both water the earth, but rain has an immediate impact while snow melts in its own time.

When I first started memorizing Scripture in an intentional, daily way, Debby assigned me some verses, and I also chose some from my daily times in God's Word (my "quiet time"). Which do you think had the most immediate impact on me? Of course—the ones from my daily quiet times! Those were the words God had used in my life that very day. Those were my "rain verses."

Sometimes the verses Debby assigned to me from lists such as The Navigators' Topical Memory System didn't make a whole lot of meaningful sense to me. Take Romans 8:32, for example:

> *He who did not spare his own Son, but gave him up for us all—how will he not also, along with him, graciously give us all things?* –Romans 8:32 (NIV)

That sounds nice. It's good truth. But it didn't penetrate my heart at the time I memorized it. When it finally "melted," it left a lifelong impact. Decades later, I can still vividly recall when that "snow verse" watered my heart. I was walking down a road at Glen Eyrie in Colorado, where I was serving for the summer in a discipleship training program. I was reviewing my verses with the help of my "verse pack"—my pack of index cards on which I wrote Scripture verses—and Romans 8:32 was among those to be reviewed that day.

I had memorized that verse almost a year earlier, but now I was going through a time of soul-searching regarding trusting the Lord for a future spouse. I wondered what "God's best" looked like for me in that area of my life. As I meditated on this verse, the truth melted into my heart: God did not even spare His own Son for me! Why would He want me to have any less than His best in an area like my life partner? If I kept following Him, He would certainly lead me to the person who would help me bring the most glory to Him, or He would affirm singleness in my life. (In my case, I ended up marrying someone I already knew and admired.)

God's Word is living and active, penetrating hearts and souls (see Hebrews 4:12). We should always include it in our times with those we are mentoring. And we should be regularly engaging with it ourselves.

Prayer

Ele Parrott, author of *Transforming Together: Authentic Spiritual Mentoring*, urges us to realize the power of prayer. "As you can see," she says, "praying is the most powerful tool we have as believers. We just don't get it, do we? It's like having an atomic bomb in our hands and playing with it as if it were a squirt gun."[2]

5. Read Matthew 18:20. What does God promise to do for those who pray together?

Jesus spoke these words within the context of unity and dealing with conflict, but the principle holds true for our prayer. There is power in believers uniting together in prayer to seek God. God's presence is there! Within these mentoring relationships, with or without conflict, we completely, unquestionably, need God in order to succeed in this ministry. Let us not neglect to give Him first place among us as we meet together in His name.

Beyond the fact that we need to invite Jesus to lead us during our times together, we need to model the essentiality of prayer in our lives and relationships in a variety of ways. I recommend you help your mentee through providing suggestions and guiding your mentee into discovering tools or practices that suit him or her. Here are some examples (others may be found in Appendix A):

- Keep prayer lists and note all answered prayers together.
- Help your mentee begin a prayer journal. It could be a place to record the lists and answered prayers, or it could be a place to actually write out prayers.
- There are phone apps that help a person develop a thriving prayer life, such as Daily Prayer App and Prayer Notes.
- Study Jesus's prayer life in God's Word.

The goal is for the mentee to develop a growing prayer life, so this growth can happen in whatever way best fits him or her. The possibilities are tremendous. Please just help your mentee to pray. It is as essential as breathing.

6. What are some other creative ways you could help your mentee develop a prayer life?

7. Which tools and methods seem most likely to suit your mentee's personality and lifestyle?

Also, pray for your mentee regularly. After all, God is the One who changes hearts. One of my earlier mentees had the great privilege of growing up in a fairly sheltered and safe home and church. She had always heard about Jesus, and she was blessed to live a life in which she didn't make any big, obvious, sinful mistakes.

The unfortunate thing about this wonderful life was that she developed a somewhat holier-than-thou attitude as well as a fear of "the world." As much as I loved and respected her, I saw this problem clearly, knew it would hinder her, and recognized it as sin. However, no matter how I tried to gently broach the topic, she was like a brick wall in this particular area. She could not see it, and she was easily offended if I tried to suggest this might be an area of needed growth. I finally resolved to relinquish it to the Lord through prayer alone. (It's too bad I didn't do that sooner!)

I faithfully prayed about this young woman's struggle for years. We eventually moved hundreds of miles apart, yet still managed to get together at least once per year. It was during one of our annual get-togethers, when she visited my family in rural North Dakota, that this mentee shared with me how God had worked in this area of her heart. She had no idea I had been praying about this need for years. I was pleased to learn that God used her desire to interact with her non-Christian coworkers to help her realize how easily she could annoy people with her sanctimonious attitude.

This Christ-follower is now spending her life sharing Jesus with people who do not know Him. Whether they have lived "holy" lives or not, she loves them and invests her time and talents in them. And she knows that it is God who enables her to do this (see 1 Corinthians 15:10).

God did the work. I simply served as the prayer intercessor.

Life

Researcher David Kinnaman, when referring to young adults leaving the church and often their Christian faith, said, "The relational element is so strong because relationship is central to disciple making—and, as we've said, the dropout problem is, at its core, a disciple-making problem."[3]

8. Return to 1 Thessalonians 2:8, this time also reading verse 7. What sort of attitude did Paul, Silvanus and Timothy have toward the Thessalonians?

Do you recognize the love between these mentors and those entrusted to their care? Effective, loving parents know about, show interest in, and invest in their children's lives.

We must find out what is going on in our mentee's life. By proving genuine interest in our mentee's life, we authenticate our care and ensure that our mentee feels like a friend rather than a project. This is how we can be relational and personal in a way that will ultimately help us in our purposefulness.

Being familiar with the happenings in your mentee's life will also help you stay relevant. Jesus demonstrated the ultimate example of relevance through His seamless use of everyday experiences in teaching His disciples. You need to observe and know what is going on in your mentee's life in order to address those things and be used by God in these areas. For example, if you are mentoring a high school student, I suggest you attend your mentee's events when possible. Your observation in a variety of settings will help you understand how your mentee lives and his or her priorities. You also will be able to address things you witness from a biblical worldview. Lest this sound too clinical, it is important to remember that this is a genuine relationship. Attending young friends' activities is a way to honor and enjoy them.

Speaker and biblical counselor Ele Parrott emphasizes partnering with who the Holy Spirit is being in the life of our mentee. This requires great prayerfulness and dependence on God rather than on our own accumulated wisdom. We watch for themes of how God is working in our mentee's life so we can partner with what He is trying to teach him or her. We should not try to detract from those things in order to stick with our own agenda. Striving for this attentiveness will help us grow too as we learn how to mentor through all aspects of life, including subjects that are newer to us. And, of course, enjoying life together is a way of showing love, which is what Jesus asks of us (see John 13:34-35).

We will get into how to balance these essentials and these approaches as we proceed through this guidebook. Of all the things you should remember from this guidebook, remember the three aspects of approach (structural, relational and personal) and the three essentials for every one-on-one (God's Word, prayer and life).

Chapter Six

A PRACTICAL PLAN
FOR A MENTORING MONTH

Now that you have a biblical foundation for spiritual mentoring, three aspects for your approach and three essentials to include in your time together, you are ready to begin with your mentee. Here are some practical steps for making the most of your time together. These suggested steps will be for mentoring pairs who aim to meet monthly. You may adapt them to your desired schedule.

A. Contact your mentee early in the month to arrange a time and place to meet. If your mentee likes structure, plan to meet at the same time regularly so you can both make it a priority in your schedules. If your mentee chafes under structure or easily feels like a project, schedule month by month. However, you do not want the seeming need for spontaneity to cause too much time to lapse between meetings. You can easily lose momentum if you do not meet at least monthly.

1. Does your mentee seem more structured or more spontaneous? If you are unsure, discuss it together. Straightforward, loving communication within a mentoring relationship is best.

2. What is your goal for how frequently you will meet? Again, make sure you and your mentee agree upon the goal.

B. A day or two before your meeting, prepare what you will cover and review your notes from last time. I keep a Word document (a Google doc or spreadsheet also would work) on each mentee. On it, I record in separate columns these items: date and meeting place, content covered, assignment for next time, prayer requests and "things to note." (I will detail more about the final item later.)

C. About one day before you meet up, it is a good idea to reconnect with your mentee to verify details about getting together (unless you have an absolutely responsible mentee who would find this annoying). Here is a sample text: "Looking forward to seeing you at the coffee shop tomorrow at 1. Can't wait to catch up!" This type of contact is also good for pre-establishing rapport, especially for those of you who are still getting used to mentoring and to each other.

D. Ideally arrive a few minutes early to your meeting place so you can warmly welcome your mentee. I like the concept of "lighting up" (your countenance, that is) when someone walks into a room, showing you care. Help your mentee see that he or she has your focused attention and interest during this time.

E. During your meeting, be sure to casually weave prayer into your time together sooner than later, asking the Lord to bless your time together. Remember these three elements overall: *God's Word*, *prayer* and *life*. You want to share about each other's lives, you want to get into the Word, and you want to pray together. "Life" also refers to making your time in the Word relevant to life.

> Basic accountability questions to ask include the following:
> - How have your quiet times been going? Can you share a highlight with me?
> - What is something new or exciting God has taught you recently?
> - Have you been memorizing any verses you want to share with me? How does that verse apply to your life?
> - Has God answered any of our prayers recently? What are you learning as you wait for God's response in that area of your life?

After providing accountability and encouragement in the basic areas of spiritual growth, get into the more structured plan you have for your time, making sure to empower your mentee to find a practical application he or she will implement. Toward the end, ask how you can pray for him or her. And then pray together (it may be only you praying aloud if your mentee is not ready for this yet).

To summarize, you will:
- Welcome your mentee and reconnect through casual conversation.
- Dedicate your time to the Lord in prayer.
- Provide some accountability in spiritual practices (e.g., daily time in God's Word, Scripture memorization, church involvement, prayer, etc.).
- Cover some original content.
- Find practical application.
- Determine "homework."
- Pray for each other.

That is a basic structure for a mentoring meeting, but there is plenty of room to adapt to your mentoring style and goals.

F. Immediately after (or subtly during) the one-on-one time together, jot down notes. Record prayer requests and continue praying for these needs. Also jot down things you should follow up on or interesting things you learned (these fall under the "things to note" column mentioned earlier). As much as you think it won't happen, it is easy to forget something that seemed so important at the time. Your mentee will appreciate your asking him or her later about something that was shared. These notes also have helped me think of gift ideas for special occasions.

G. Throughout the month, pray daily for your mentee. Pray for yourself, that you would depend on the Holy Spirit to guide you during your preparations and during your time together. You and I are totally dependent on God to make the most of these relationships and times together.

3. How do you plan to incorporate daily prayer for your mentee into your schedule?

H. Remember that you are not limited to one meeting per month. Many mentoring pairs meet twice per month, weekly, or whenever the need/desire arises. If possible, do casual, fun activities together too, simply as an indication that you care about more than just your formal meetings. Doing something active or hands-on together can loosen up both of you, which will help conversation flow more freely.

4. What interests do you share with your mentee?

5. What activities could you participate in or attend together?

How you spend your time may vary somewhat from meeting to meeting. If your mentee is dealing with something particularly difficult, you may choose to focus your time on praying together. If you are both very interested in or perplexed by part of your Bible reading, you may choose to really dig into a particular passage, even using additional tools (e.g., commentary, concordance and/or Bible dictionary). If your mentee has posed a deep and pertinent question, you may need to dig into that topic (ideally using the Bible as your guide and praying for wisdom and understanding). Many people go through a Bible study or book together as their main content for each meeting. The Navigators' *Design for Discipleship* series is a good example of a relevant study series. (You will find more suggestions at the end of Appendix A.)

6. What initial ideas do you have for material to cover during your mentoring meetings?

It may take a little time to establish a routine with your mentee, but be patient. You will find the rhythms that best fit your mentoring relationship.

Chapter Seven

HELPFUL TIPS FOR NEW MENTORS

Effective mentoring is learned through experience and maturity, but following are some practical tips you will find helpful.

A. **Communicate continually.** Periodically check in on expectations. At one point, I noticed a trend within the mentoring program I coordinate. A higher proportion of first-year students wanted new mentors at the end of their first year, in stark contrast to very few upper-level students seeking new mentors. Upon further investigation, I concluded that these younger students were hearing wonderful stories about other students and mentors who had been together for more years. They were feeling like their relationships didn't measure up. The younger students hadn't taken into consideration that the other students and mentors had been developing rapport and trust over several years.

If something seems amiss, it is important to discuss it. This is a relationship. People have expectations—and sometimes they are not even consciously aware of those expectations. Talk through expectations, concerns, dreams and desires so you and your mentee can move forward on the same page.

1. What expectations have you and your mentee already discussed?

2. What are some topics you should discuss soon?

B. Be real with your mentee, but use discretion. It is crucial to be authentic in these relationships, but you also need to keep maturity in mind. Some mentees are mature enough to accept you despite your weaknesses, and some might benefit from more general language in terms of your own imperfections. This is not only for your own relational dynamics—it is also to avoid mentees justifying making the same mistakes you made because you turned out "just fine."

C. Make sure not to monopolize your time together. Even though you want to impart what God has given you, you don't want to make this all about you. If you are regularly doing most of the talking, you need to evaluate why that keeps happening. Perhaps your mentee needs greater pauses in conversation before he or she will speak. Silence can compel conversation.

D. Regularly evaluate your progress. Ask yourself questions such as these: "Am I seeing fruit in both our lives? Are other lives being impacted through us? Are we moving forward, or are we getting bogged down by distractions? Has my mentee been taught what to do and how to do it?"

Assess your relationship through Scripture. Ask yourself, Are we moving toward 1 Timothy 1:5? Am I doing 1 Thessalonians 5:14? Is our relationship reflecting Hebrews 10:24-25?

At one point I discovered that I was spending so much time discussing life with a certain mentee that we were not getting much time in the Word together. I started opening God's Word earlier, and there was no lack in discussing the more personal areas of our lives. I find that getting into God's living, active Word (as it is described in Hebrews 4:12) naturally lends itself to life application and sharing with one another.

E. Provide gentle instruction in areas of weakness. Few people crave correction, but it is foolish to hate it, according to Proverbs 12:1. It is difficult to find someone who will actually help us see our faults and work on them. But correction is truly a gift that teachable people appreciate in the long run (see Proverbs 13:18).

Let me give one common example. Many people avoid discussing purity, especially within specific relationships. I have run across countless young people who have been in dating relationships and longing for someone to provide accountability and encouragement in purity. Even the most God-focused couples battle against their God-given hormones. A mentor willing to calmly and graciously discuss this topic provides a great gift. An alternative is to suggest, "I may not be the right person to hold you accountable in this area, but tell me someone who is. Then I will hold you accountable to asking that person, and I'll occasionally ask if you are still receiving the accountability you desire in this area."

F. Teach how to fish; don't give a fish. Just as Isaiah 55:10-11 talks about God's Word being like bread (to eat now) and seed (to use for longer-term results), we want to not just provide for immediate needs, but also to equip our mentees for future fruitful ministry and an abundant life. We also can consider 2 Timothy 2:2 again: Paul did not only invest in Timothy, but he also urged Timothy to invest in other men who would be qualified to equip still more men.

G. Make the most of your casual times together. Even while participating in lighter activities, you may casually weave God's Word, prayer and life into your conversation. You may ask what the mentee is learning from the Bible, you may share a verse you've memorized or something God has been doing in your life, or you may suggest pausing to pray about a topic you're discussing. Doing so models the significance of God's Word and prayer in daily life, including mundane and casual activities!

H. Take the right initiative. With younger mentees (i.e., high school students), you will probably have to take more initiative in your relationship (e.g., calling, setting up times, reminding about assignments, etc.). Gradually ease the greater responsibility in the mentee's direction as you meet together over a more extended period of time.

I. Be conscientious in choosing your meeting places. While mentoring relationships are most effective when mentees can open up about personal and heartfelt topics, you also need to be above reproach in these relationships, including the situations in which you place yourself and your mentee. Be wise, and please communicate with your mentee (and his or her parents if your mentee is a high school student) about his or her expectations regarding time alone together, traveling in vehicles, etc. An ideal meeting place will involve enough distance that you won't be concerned about people overhearing you, yet you will be visible to others.

3. What are some good options for meeting places that will be appropriate and convenient for both of you?

J. Mentees may forget things, even your meeting times. These things happen, with some personalities more than others. Do not assume your mentee doesn't value you or your time together. This is simply a good reason to call or text the day before your scheduled meeting to confirm details. If missing meetings becomes a pattern, it is worth addressing as an area of growth for which you can provide guidance.

K. Intentionally work on helping your mentee develop consistency in pursuing Christ through the spiritual disciplines. Pray that God will help you be a master teacher of the tools needed to grow, such as daily quiet times, Scripture memorization and prayer. (This topic will be explored further in the following chapters.)

L. Do not lose sight of the greater vision. As mentioned in Chapter Three, Christ-followers tend to gravitate toward evangelism *or* mentoring/discipleship. As your mentoring relationship deepens, you may get caught up in enjoying each other and what God is doing in both of you. Regularly remind yourself that this relationship needs to overflow into others' lives—through mentoring other believers, but also through sharing the good news about Jesus Christ with those who do not yet have a relationship with Him. You have been commissioned to reach the world for Christ!

Chapter Eight
THE VALUE
AND POTENTIAL OF ONE

Now that you have reached this point, you hopefully have been convinced that there is a biblical mandate for spiritual mentoring and have realized mentoring's significance. You also have learned some specific things about how to approach mentoring relationships and how to effectively conduct them. Take some time here to dig a little deeper into the value of the person you are mentoring. God's Word has some exciting things to say on this topic. (As with all verses in this guidebook, I encourage you to eventually take a deeper look at these verses and passages within their greater context. There is so much more to be learned!)

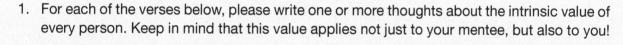

1. For each of the verses below, please write one or more thoughts about the intrinsic value of every person. Keep in mind that this value applies not just to your mentee, but also to you!

   a. Genesis 1:26

   b. Psalm 100:3

   c. Jeremiah 29:11

   d. John 3:16

   e. 2 Peter 3:9

2. Please summarize what you have gleaned about the worth of each individual in God's sight.

3. For each of the following verses or passages, please note something that God has done through one person. If you are already familiar with these passages, don't let familiarity hinder you from the wonder and vision to be gained from these stories.

   a. Genesis 1:28-30

   b. Exodus 3:1-10

   c. Jeremiah 5:1

   d. Mark 1:1-8

   e. Galatians 4:4-5 (I'm hinting at the person mentioned who is not Jesus.)

4. Considering all of the stories in these passages, what sort of potential does every person have in the service of Almighty God?

In your mind, is the significance of this biblical truth translating to your mentoring relationship? That sheepish young man with his hair in his face may very well save a city or nation someday! That woman who sometimes seems a little obnoxious to you now may risk her life in a country where the gospel is not welcome. Or *you* may.

5. Take a moment to prayerfully consider this information and to write out a prayer for your mentee. Pray about what you desire to see God do in his or her life. Pray about your willingness to be used by Him as part of the process.

Chapter Nine

THE BEST WAY
TO HELP YOUR MENTEE

A favorite verse of mine is Psalm 90:12: "Teach us to number our days, that we may gain a heart of wisdom" (NIV). We do not know how much time we have with our mentee. We only know that our mentee is valuable and that God wants us to make the most of the limited time we have (see Ephesians 5:16). I met with one woman on a weekly basis for a couple of years, and then suddenly she was getting married and moving to Massachusetts in a few short months! I asked God, "Did I make the most of the time I had?" At that point, I sure hoped so, since the time I had left with her was coming to an end. There was no time for a do-over.

There is great value in continually reminding ourselves of our purpose as well as of our timeframe. I like to give myself goals for certain time periods (e.g., "I would like to see her having a consistent daily quiet time by the end of the summer"). Setting small goals can help keep us on track. However, we need to remember that we do not want our goals to start feeling like "project deadlines." (Go back and read Chapter Four again if necessary.)

A good understanding of how we can best help is crucial. After all, keep in mind the potential we're dealing with (the big goal)! Envision those x's that illustrate spiritual multiplication (see Chapter Three).

As you evaluate how you can best help, here are some questions to prayerfully consider. Please jot down your initial responses.

1. What is the difference between teaching and equipping?

2. Which is harder to find?

3. Which is harder to do?

4. Which has a longer-term impact and why?

We can certainly argue that good teaching is equipping, but the point is not so much to dispute semantics as it is to develop a vision for how we can best invest in our mentees. There is no limit to the number of things we can teach. In fact, our mentees can tap into seemingly unlimited resources through churches, Bible studies, classes, media (including books, the internet, podcasts, streaming, etc.) and more. Their phones alone might seem to have all they need.

A good question to ask is, "If God were to send my mentees to pioneer an international or domestic mission field where there will not be a spiritual support network, what can I do to best set them up to succeed?" I use a somewhat extreme example here because it clearly illustrates the point. The reality is that we want the tools we provide to be incredibly helpful wherever the Lord leads our mentees.

5. About that idea of pioneering a mission field... If you were sent to an isolated place where you weren't guaranteed fellowship or spiritual leadership, what would you most want to have spiritually? In other words, how would you most want to be equipped?

Although specific topics such as how to manage your money, how to stay pure in a sex-saturated culture, or how to develop meaningful friendships are good and important subjects, these and other random topics may not determine whether or not you survive and thrive in your mission field. How much better would you serve your mentees by not necessarily providing them with answers to these specific concerns, but by preparing them to find these answers on their own?

6. Who is someone to whom you feel you can go for godly guidance?

7. What is it about that person that draws you to him or her?

It's generally the people of the Word, people who are attuned to God's direction through a well-developed prayer life, those walking with Jesus in an evident way, those experiencing His power in their lives—these are the people to whom we turn. We can attain these attributes as well—and help our mentees do the same. This should be our prayerful goal.

Robert Coleman wrote about this truth in *The Master Plan of Evangelism*. He said, "His [Jesus's] method was to get the disciples into a vital experience with God, and to show them how he worked, before telling them they had to do it."[1]

So, as we consider this aspect of our mentoring relationships, we turn again to some fundamentals that help us and our mentees develop vital relationships with God.

Read the Bible and pray.

In my junior high years at church, my friend Wilfredo would jokingly give the same answer every time he was called upon by a leader: "Read the Bible and pray." He would offer the same silly grin each time, indicating that he wasn't taking things too seriously. However, the older both he and I have gotten, the more we've realized the wisdom of those words.

A vital experience with God comes through a very intimate relationship with Him. I often use a simple illustration called the Communication Circle to show how we can strengthen our relationship with God.

The Communication Circle

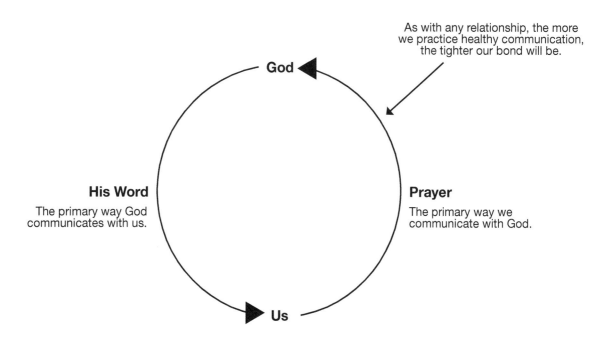

As with any relationship, the more we practice healthy communication, the tighter our bond will be.

God

His Word
The primary way God communicates with us.

Prayer
The primary way we communicate with God.

Us

When I use this illustration while teaching a group, I talk about different kinds of mother-son relationships. I sometimes even have people act out these relationships. The scenarios could look like this:

- One son comes home from school and chatters incessantly, not letting his mother get a word in edgewise.
- Another son arrives home from school and his mother can't get a word out of him, no matter how hard she tries. He responds with unintelligible grunts and shrugs.
- The final mother-son pair has a healthy interaction, with each attentively listening and appropriately responding.

These are examples of how we might relate with God as we approach Him. Do we bombard Him with our needs and requests without taking any time to hear what He has to say? Are we open to God's Word being taught to us at church and perhaps even through personal reading, but do not bother to respond back to the Lord through prayer?

The Communication Circle can not only illustrate how our relationship with God needs to involve two-way communication, but also help to demonstrate how to have a quiet time:

- Prayerfully enter God's presence, asking Him to teach you.
- Listen to Him as He instructs you through His Word.
- Respond to what He shares with you, prayerfully discussing how you can apply it to your life and thanking Him for revealing truth to you.

Finally, in a broader sense, the Communication Circle shows how we need to be communicating with God throughout each day. The fundamentals of this circle are listening to Him primarily through His Word and communicating with Him through prayer.

Just read the Bible and pray? Yes, but this simple formula is not always so simply followed. For example, how long did it take for you to develop good habits in communicating with and listening to God each day? What were the circumstances that brought you to that point?

8. How are you really doing at this point in your life with spending time in the Word and prayer each day?

We should be asking ourselves this question: "How can I equip my mentees so that the most basic elements of a thriving spiritual life become nonnegotiable for them?" If we allow God to use us in leading them to that place, they will likely develop a strong spiritual hunger and be set up to walk in obedience. They will be able to seek answers and guide others.

It sometimes feels like those we mentor probably already "know" those things. Well, the way of testing that thought is to discern whether the mentees are actually practicing them. If they're not, they really *don't* get it (or they are rebelling in these areas, which we hope is not the case). If they don't get it, we should pray and ask ourselves what we can do to lead our mentee there. What other passage should we explore? What other biblical illustration can we use? What story from our or someone else's life will motivate them?

Let's take a moment to brainstorm on these topics.

9. What are some of the best tools you know that may motivate your mentee to get into the Word?

10. What are some of the best tools you have to help your mentee develop his or her prayer life?

Ask yourself what has worked best for you and for others you respect.

Following are some ideas you may or may not have already considered. Many of these resources may be found in Appendix A of this guidebook. Many of them also may be found through a brief internet search.

Regarding the Word
How and why to have a daily quiet time:
- Communication Circle
- "7 Minutes with God" pamphlet by Robert D. Foster
- Luke 10:38-42
- YouVersion[2] or another Bible app
- Ephesians 6:10-18
- Exodus 16

How to study the Bible:
- *Living By the Book* by Howard Hendricks and William Hendricks
- "Observation, Interpretation, Application" or OIA, an in-depth Bible study method (search online for more information)
- Chapter 3 of *By the Word of God* by Tom Harmon

How to memorize Scripture:
- *Memorize This: TMS 3.0* by D. Mason Rutledge
- *You Need to Memorize Scripture* by N. A. Woychuk
- Chapter 4 of *By the Word of God* by Tom Harmon

How to meditate on and apply Scripture:
- Verse Analysis: A Meditation Study (found in Appendix A)
- 4 P's of meditation (see the Sample Lesson Plan, "Meditation/Application" in Appendix A)
- "The Word Hand" (a Navigators resource found online that illustrates the importance of hearing, reading, studying, memorizing and meditating on Scripture)
- Chapter 5 of *By the Word of God* by Tom Harmon

Regarding prayer

- "The Prayer Hand" (a Navigators resource found online that illustrates the importance of confession, petition, intercession, thanksgiving and praise)
- ACTS—Adoration/Confession/Thanksgiving/Supplication (see "ACTS": A Prayer Study in Appendix A)
- Operation World[3] (an online resource for praying for nations)
- *The Practice of the Presence of God* by Brother Lawrence
- Praying Scripture (see the Sample Lesson Plan, "Praying Scripture" in Appendix A)
- The Lord's Prayer
- Recognizing the prayerfulness of worship songs through some time of actual worship and looking at lyrics
- A prayer journal
- Claiming God's promises, etc.

I have developed the habit of accumulating good resources. I encourage you to start a computer file, notes app, three-ring binder and/or file box to organize these resources. If I hear a good sermon on a topic I use in mentoring, I file it appropriately. If I read a good article…same thing. If I do a good Bible study on a pertinent topic, I make note of it in the corresponding file. In this way, I have accumulated helpful resources that I can turn to when I recognize a need in a mentee—or when someone asks for help with a particular concern.

Again, we cannot underestimate the power of prayer. We need to be seeking God's help first as we try to help our mentees develop intimacy with Him.

11. Read Joshua 9 and jot down a summary of the events.

12. On what basis did the Israelites make their decision?

13. What key mistake did the Israelites make in verse 14?

14. What were the long-term consequences for this oversight?

Seeking God's guidance in our mentoring relationships is essential, and we need to both teach and model that.

Effectively drawing your mentee into a vital relationship with God is going to involve not only prayer, but also practical encouragement through accountability. Feel free to give assignments, whether that involves asking your mentee to have a certain number of quiet times, including writing down the application point; or whether that involves asking him or her to memorize verses. You will want to hold your mentee accountable to the basic spiritual practices with each one-to-one meeting.

However, along with providing accountability, we need to be sure we are mentoring within an environment of grace. Scott Morton's book *Down to Earth Discipling* has a whole chapter on this topic. Morton wrote that "when you teach high biblical standards in discipleship (which you should)…you are in danger of a 'push-back' toward legalism."[4]

Here is another related statement from the book to consider:

> We can overchallenge our conscientious mentorees in small groups or in one-to-one discipling. We usually feel more useful if we give a challenging sermonette (usually to pray more or to share Christ more). One of the guys I'm discipling calls that "pounding"! It's easier to pound than to genuinely encourage. Your mentorees who come from a crushing dysfunctional background can't handle pounding!
>
> But Jesus goes further. What does the leader do to help the pupils carry the load? The Pharisees would not lift a finger. These days, if I give a heavy challenge, I offer resources. For example, when challenging people to have a daily quiet time, I give them "Seven Minutes with God" from NavPress or my paragraph-a-day outline of Mark's gospel.[5]

Some of us might tend toward "pounding." Some of us might tend toward never wanting to challenge our mentees at all because that might be uncomfortable. Each of us could benefit from some prayerful observation of our own styles and our mentees' responses.

15. Do you tend toward "pounding" or toward holding back with accountability and exhortation?

Putting in the effort of studying these dynamics is worthwhile, as is being intentional with the precious time we have with our mentees. After all, helping to develop a vital relationship with God is the greatest gift we can give our mentees, and those vital relationships will ultimately help impact and reach the world for Christ.

Yet, as helpful as tools, disciplines and practices may be, we need to know—and help our mentees know—that God is not going to love us any more because of what we are doing for Him. God will not love us more if we have more quiet times, join more Bible studies, lengthen our prayer times, or memorize verses. He loves us perfectly right now.

God looks at our hearts. What these practices show Him is our heart to know Him. By pursuing God through spiritual practices, we get to know Him better—who He is and how He thinks. We grow spiritually healthier. After all, it is healthier to eat than to not eat. We will be healthier if we consume His Word (see Matthew 4:4).

As we train, encourage and equip mentees, we should regularly remind them that God loves them perfectly right now. Nothing will change that.

Chapter Ten
ATTITUDES IN MENTORING

Let's recap. We are reaching the world through one-on-one relationships. We are keenly aware of the intrinsic value and potential of each person God has made, so we are doing our best to fully equip our mentees for whatever God has in store for them. We know this intention involves developing vital relationships with God, so we are structurally, relationally and personally approaching these mentoring relationships. We always include God's Word, prayer and life in our times together, and we are accumulating resources that will provide us with ways to help our mentees develop intimacy with Christ and be prepared to help others do the same.

As we near the end of this guidebook and begin to feel more confident in the ministry that lies ahead, let us now take a look at some attitudes we need to nurture as we minister to others.

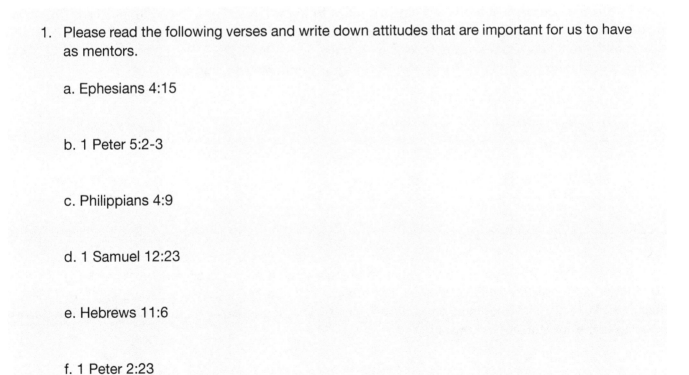

1. Please read the following verses and write down attitudes that are important for us to have as mentors.

    a. Ephesians 4:15

    b. 1 Peter 5:2-3

    c. Philippians 4:9

    d. 1 Samuel 12:23

    e. Hebrews 11:6

    f. 1 Peter 2:23

I believe it is important to acknowledge that a mentor may experience suffering while investing in someone else. I like people to know this in advance so it does not derail them and so they can focus on responding as Christ did. Here are the three forms of suffering I most often see in mentoring relationships:

- There is the suffering you experience when you grieve with those you love. Hard things happen. In my first decade of leading a mentoring program for high school students, twelve students lost a parent to death—often unexpectedly. When you love someone, you grieve and suffer alongside that person. As a mentor, your role is to be available during this time and to continue pointing toward hope.

- You also suffer when those who are dear to you and in whom you've invested so much time and energy make poor choices. Along with the pain of watching this happen, you also may wonder whether you failed your mentee in some way. Allow yourself to grieve and process, but your response during this time also will help determine the long-term success of the relationship. I have heard more than one mentor share stories of their mentee "testing" them by saying they got their girlfriend pregnant (which was not true) to see whether their mentor would still love and make time for them.

- Finally, you may find yourself suffering as you are betrayed by the very ones for whom you have given yourself. Think of Jesus, who poured into Judas as one of His disciples, knowing the entire time that Judas would ultimately betray Him. Believe it or not, I have seen similar situations unfold more than once for people mentoring high school students with insecure parents. In those cases, the parents began to feel jealous of the mentors and sought to undermine the mentors in their children's minds. In some cases, the parent outright fabricated terrible stories about the mentors, who were then criticized and "dumped" by the mentees. In most cases, the mentee eventually came back to the mentor to apologize, but it often took years of living independently before the mentee saw the situation clearly.

All of these scenarios of suffering are opportunities to know Christ more (see Philippians 3:10). These are opportunities to have faith that God can take a bad thing and use it for His glory (see Romans 8:28-29). Again, we try to follow Christ's example, as demonstrated in 1 Peter 2:23.

What attitudes do you find in the following Scriptures? Continue your study.

g. Galatians 6:9-10

h. John 13:34-35

I end this section with love, for we are to put on love above all other virtues (see Colossians 3:14). We seek love more than we seek spiritual gifts (see 1 Corinthians 14:1 and 13:2). Love is what remains (see 1 Corinthians 13:13). May we love our mentees as close to Christ's love as possible. And may the world see God's love reflected in our mentoring relationships.

Chapter Eleven
HOW TO FIND A MENTEE

There are two ways to approach the process of finding a mentee: organically or formally. The organic approach almost always works best with today's young adults and teens, but let's explore both.

Organic

1. What do you think of when you hear the word "organic"?

People—especially younger people—like things to happen naturally. The strong desire for authenticity is a big part of this preference. They want relationships to develop in a way that proves the person is genuinely interested in them. So, our ideal mentee would be someone who seems to already respect us and enjoy our input regarding his or her life.

2. Who is someone in your life who already seems to turn to you for advice or encourage-ment? (I suggest only listing names of the same sex because men mentoring women and vice versa can get quite complicated.) List more than one name if multiple people fit this description.

3. Of the people listed for the preceding question, whose company do you enjoy the most? Or which person, when spending time with that person, causes you to feel most fulfilled? Why?

A mentoring pair should feel a certain level of chemistry. Both the mentor and the mentee should like one another and enjoy each other's company. Things will proceed with more consistency and enjoyment if you both benefit from and look forward to your times together.

Formal

If names don't come to mind when considering the questions in the former section, you could tie in with a group that will enable you to create these types of relationships. Some possibilities include the following:

- **Your church.** There are often several opportunities within churches to offer help to someone who is newer to the faith than you. Here are some examples:
  - Small groups
  - Youth group
  - New believers whom a church leader knows need mentoring
  - People who have recently been baptized
- **Your alma mater.** It is not uncommon for college graduates to help with a campus ministry or Bible study group that provided them with growth opportunities when they were students. Talk with a leader and see if your volunteer help would meet a need.
- **A community organization.** There are national nonprofits like Big Brothers Big Sisters of America and local organizations like Best Kids that crave your involvement. MENTOR National offers resources and connects people with mentoring organizations. Please note that, depending on the organization's mission and guidelines, these programs may limit your spiritual emphasis. Be sure to research whether the group will be a good fit for you before you commit.
- **Your family.** You may have nieces, nephews, cousins or younger siblings who could use some extra care and guidance.

4. Which of these more formal options seems to best fit your situation?

Some organizations may assign a mentee, while others provide opportunities for relationships to naturally develop (as described in the organic section above). Regardless, *you should pray* for God to show you whom He wants you to mentor. There are more people out there who would benefit from a mentor than there are people who are willing to serve as mentors. Someone is ready for you to take this role in his or her life.

Once you identify a person who might be a good mentee, simply ask that person whether he or she would like to meet for coffee (or whatever seems most appropriate). During that time together, ask this person to share his or her story. Specific questions to ask could include these:

- How did you hear about God?
- What are some highs and lows from your life?
- What have been some key turning points in your life and faith?
- Is there an area where God is challenging you to grow right now?
- What are some ways you pursue God in your daily life?

Additionally, here is what author and mentor Jeff Myers describes as the magic sentence: "Tell me more about that."[1] Using that sentence or some variation of it will draw out your potential mentee, hopefully leading to an interesting and insightful conversation.

If it seems there is potential for you to speak into this person's life in the future, say, "Let's do this again sometime," and see what his or her response is. If this person seems eager, then do your part to follow up later.

After a couple of meetings together, suggest that perhaps you could get together regularly. Offer that you'd be willing to mentor him or her if the person is interested, making sure to mention how you benefit from what the other individual offers as well. If he or she seems uncertain, suggest a trial period of three to six months to see if mentoring turns out to be something that adds value to both of your lives.

Chapter Twelve
CLOSING THOUGHTS

A s we wrap things up, let me share another verse:

The one who calls you is faithful, and he will do it. –1 Thessalonians 5:24 (NIV)

As Debby says, "You always have time for one. For the rest of your life, you have time for one. Even when young children are clamoring about your feet, they need to see Mom or Dad reaching out to people, bringing them to Jesus. For your own mental health, get your eyes off of yourself and onto the needs of the world. You always have time for one."

God is with us. God wants us to know and experience Him more fully as we invest in a brother or sister in His family. He glorifies Himself through our weaknesses (see 2 Corinthians 12:9). It is for His glory that these mentoring relationships succeed.

So…go for it! Pour your life and what you have learned into others—who will reach still more people. Remember, there are almost eight billion souls in this big, glorious world, and billions of them are still unreached. Spiritual multiplication is the way you and I will reach them.

And the things you have heard me say in the presence of many witnesses entrust to reliable men who will also be qualified to teach others. –2 Timothy 2:2 (NIV)

What is your next step?

ACKNOWLEDGMENTS

Special Thanks

This training guidebook for mentors would not be possible without the loving, intentional spiritual investment of Lee and Debby Maschhoff. This godly couple has modeled and taught this type of ministry not only to my husband and me, but also to generations of Christ-followers.

Thank you, Lee and Debby.

As is fitting with the message of this book, I would also like to thank those who intentionally invested in Debby. Nancy Advocaat, Virginia DeHaan and Dottie Anderson are Debby's spiritual mothers, making them my spiritual grandmothers.

Additional Thanks

Dennis Derdoski, Ann Fadden, Jeanne Pride, Steve Rice and Emily Zemacke provided practical help through serving as test readers of the Barnabas program edition.

Jeanette Biesecker, Stacy Brooks, Luis Chavez, Paul Choh, Chad Dumas, Gina Hott, Maria Jun, Nathaniel Knoll, Abigail Lance, Jennifer Miller, Tina Nunemaker, Winter Saunders and Brandi South provided invaluable feedback as test readers and "fresh eyes" for this edition.

Hundreds of mentors tested and implemented the material through their participation in Joy El Generation's Barnabas mentoring program.

Thank you, Tom Yeakley, for freely sharing your "Walking by Faith with the Promises of God" resource. Check out his book, *Praying Over God's Promises*, to learn more about this topic.

My husband, Aaron Ziebarth, was primary in making sure this project happened. Marsha Blessing of Orison Publishers and her team helped me cross the finish line.

Appendix A
MENTORING RESOURCES AND SAMPLE LESSONS

GROW ACROSTIC

The GROW acrostic, which is widely used in professional coaching circles, helps you guide your mentee in a specific area of desired growth. This tool may be used in countless situations, including working toward a goal or improving a spiritual practice. You should work through these steps with your mentee.

Goal   Determine what the ideal situation would be.

Reality   Analyze the difference between that ideal and the present reality.

Options   Discuss how to get from reality to ideal. "How can we get from here to there?" List as many options as possible, ranging from silly to practical.

Walk   Turn the options into realistic action steps. Talk with your mentee. "We want to narrow these down to our best ideas and then use one at a time. Are there any we can immediately eliminate? Which ideas seem most compelling to you? Which one is most realistic to try in the very near future? How can you specifically begin putting this plan into practice this week?" Make preparations to follow up on your action plan, then return to try a new idea in the future if that would be helpful.

The following are sample lesson plans for key areas of instruction. I created all of these lesson plans for my own use as a mentor. Appendix B tells you how to write your own lesson plans. Note that you can use phrases for brevity rather than writing out complete sentences.

Sample Lesson Plan
Quiet Time: Exodus 16
(Created from material taught by Debby Maschhoff)

Objective: That the mentee would be motivated to meet with God and eat His Word daily.

Plan:
1. Pray.
2. Read Exodus 16:1-3. Looking backward toward Egypt and blaming Moses. Forgetting what it was really like. Emphasize v. 4: go out each day and gather enough for the day.
3. Connect with Old Testament (OT). Must look at OT through New Testament eyes.
4. Refer to John 6:33, 48-51. Who is the bread? Jesus is the bread!
5. Refer to Matthew 4:4. What is the bread? The Word is the bread! "What is it?" in Hebrew=Manna.
6. Return to Exodus 16:4 and discuss what it means for us now. Emphasize every day and enough for that day. Why did God want them to gather every day? To prove His faithfulness and to see if they would walk in His ways: obedience!
7. Read vv. 5-8. Murmuring and grumbling is always against the Lord—you do not like how He is handling your life. Verse 6: Get fed in a supernatural way—a sign God is working in you. Same with daily quiet time: not just look to get through but a supernatural feeding.
8. Read vv. 9-12. Moses told them, "In the morning you will be filled…" (NIV). They still didn't recognize it. Moses had never seen it before either, and yet he knew what it was. He believed God's Word. He had no preconceived notions about what it would look like, etc. He just believed it was bread from God; it was a supernatural feeding.
9. Read vv. 13-15: "It is the bread!" Are we going to be a Moses or like the people of Israel? It is our choice.
10. Continue reading Exodus 16. Verse 15: Israelites cry, "What is it?" They did not recognize it as bread; it was not what they pictured or expected. But it is what God chose for them and how He was going to feed them. Verse 16: you are to take only what you need. Some took a lot, some a little; either was enough. God knows what we need. It is not the same for everyone. What we take we must use—apply to our lives! Verse 20: Some took much but didn't use it. It turned wormy and was counterproductive. Same with us if we do not apply God's Word. Don't just take things in—apply it! Verses 31-33: Things about manna: white (pure), seed (multiplication capabilities), sweet (same as the Word in Psalm 119:103). Verse 32: save some for generations to come. The Word—we need to share it with our following generations. Memorials. Verse 35: keep feeding on it until Canaan. (We won't have arrived until then!) Might get dull at times (doesn't need to be!), but keep on until heaven.
11. Read Psalm 78:23-25. They ate the bread of angels in heaven.
12. Discuss how the mentee is doing on quiet times. How he or she can apply this passage.
13. Pray.

Other Resources:
- Luke 10
- "The Word Hand" (a Navigators resource found online)
- "The Wheel" (a Navigators resource found online)
- *Manna in the Morning* booklet by Stephen F. Olford

Sample Lesson Plan
Scripture Memory

Objective: To motivate mentee to develop intimacy with Jesus and effectiveness in ministry through the memorization of Scripture.

Plan:
1. Pray.
2. Ask mentee about his or her experience with and thoughts on Scripture memorization.
3. Share a powerful Scripture memorization story with him or her.
4. Look through the following verses together:
   - Romans 12:1-2
   - Psalm 119:9-11
   - Isaiah 55:10-11
   - Jeremiah 15:16
   - Jeremiah 20:9
   - John 14:21
5. Talk about next steps for him or her, possibly teaching the "verse pack" system.
6. Pray.

Other Resources:
- Matthew 4, Luke 4 and Jesus's example
- Topical Memory System*
- *You Need to Memorize Scripture* by N. A. Woychuk and/or accompanying Scripture Memory Fellowship app
- Charlotte Mason memorization system
- *Memorize This* by D. Mason Rutledge
- Bethlehem Baptist Church's Fighter Verses program and/or accompanying Fighter Verses app
- Other Bible memorization apps, such as the Bible Memory app; Bible Memory by MemLok; Remember Me; or Verses – Bible Memory

*I have been memorizing and meditating on Scripture for my entire adult life, successfully using the Topical Memory System. Using this system requires acquiring a verse pack, which is a pack of Scripture cards as well as a verse card holder to place those cards into. You can find these on Etsy, by calling Joy El Camps & Retreats at 717-369-4539, or through the Glen Eyrie bookstore (https://gleneyriebookstore.org/). Pay attention to size before you purchase. Or you can make your own Scripture memorization cards by writing verses on index cards.

"ACTS"
A Prayer Study

The ACTS acrostic—adoration, confession, thanksgiving and supplication—is often used to help people broaden their prayer lives. I designed this study to provide scriptural support and examples of the different facets of prayer from the acrostic. After examining the Scriptures related to each facet, practice this type of prayer together.

A. Adoration
    1. Support: Psalm 150
        Psalm 148:11-14
    2. Sample: Psalm 145:1-9
    3. Practice:

B. Confession
    1. Support: Psalm 66:18
        Psalm 24:3-5
    2. Sample: Psalm 51:1-3
    3. Practice:

C. Thanksgiving
    1. Support: Psalm 106:1
        1 Thessalonians 5:18
    2. Sample: Daniel 2:23
    3. Practice:

D. Supplication
    1. Support: Philippians 4:6-7
        Ephesians 6:18
    2. Sample: Daniel 9:15-19
    3. Practice:

Application

Sample Lesson Plan
Praying Scripture

As we discussed in Chapter Seven, helping your mentee rely on Christ is an essential part of mentoring. This lesson plan is a tool you can use to help mentees build their prayer life and Scripture memorization.

Objective: To help the mentee see the value in praying Scripture to develop intimacy with Jesus, as well as providing tools to develop the skill.

Plan:

I. Pray.

II. Lay the foundation:
 A. If we worship God through singing Scripture, why not worship Him through praying it? The Psalms have been a prayer book for public and private worship for centuries, used by some churches more than others, but valid for all believers.
 B. It is an exercise for bringing Bible reading and prayer together. Refer to the Communication Circle (see Chapter Nine).
 C. Benefits:
  1. Keeps our prayer life fresh.
  2. Reminds us who God is, what He has done, and what He will/can do.
  3. Brings the Bible to life.
  4. Internalizes memorized Scripture.
  5. Helps us in claiming promises.
 D. "When you pray with Scripture the Word becomes flesh in us embodied in service." –Kent Ira Goff[1]

III. Definitions:
 A. "'Praying Scripture' is using passages of Scripture to stimulate prayer or when we say verses directly back to God, making them the petition of our hearts." –Lance Witt, founder of Replenish Ministries[2]
 B. *Lectio divina*: "The 'divine' or 'prayerful' reading of Scriptures. Read a short text prayerfully—over and over, like a cow chewing her cud—until you are led to 'delight in God.'" –Benedict of the 5th Century, as quoted by Goff in *The Soul of Tomorrow's Church*[3]

IV. *An application/learning from the cow:
 A. Read. Silently, aloud or both. *Graze.*
 B. Meditate. Reread. Ponder context. Think about meanings. *Chew the fresh grass.*
 C. Pray. Let the text get into your gut and connect with your feelings. *Ruminate/Regurgitate the cud.*
 D. Contemplate. Allow the Word to get into your bloodstream. *Rest and digest.*
 –Contributed by Guigo II, who said this should begin with silence; also quoted by Goff in *The Soul of Tomorrow's Church*.[4]

V. Practice praying Scripture with one or all of the following:
 • Revelation 5:9-14
 • Ephesians 1:15-19
 • Psalm 119:9-24
 • Deuteronomy 32:3-4
 • Psalm 42:1-5, if discouraged

VI. Homework: Most likely trying the Guigo II form (see section IV) of praying Scripture with an area where he or she is reading now or with a recommended passage.

Other Resources:
- *Praying Over God's Promises* by Tom Yeakley
- "Walking by Faith with the Promises of God" handout by Tom Yeakley (included in this appendix)
- Chapter 5 of *Developing Your Secret Closet of Prayer* by Richard Burr
- *Praying God's Word* by Beth Moore
- *Praying the Lord's Prayer for Spiritual Breakthrough* by Elmer Towns
- *The Soul of Tomorrow's Church* by Kent Ira Goff
- Lots of practice reading verses and praying in response together

*Omit these portions if the plan needs to be shortened and/or simplified, or if meeting with a teen.

Sample Lesson Plan
Fellowship

Objective: To identify relational principles as taught through Scripture, helping the mentee aim for relationships that strengthen his or her intimacy with Jesus.

Plan:

1. Chat, touching on relationships, asking about current fellowship situation.
2. Pray.
3. Look through relational verses at the end of this lesson plan, focusing on ones most applicable to his or her situation.
4. Ask how his or her primary relationships can be defined when evaluated by these Scriptures.
5. Go through 1 John 1:1-4 to take a good look at what Christ-centered fellowship should look like.
6. Ask the mentee what application he or she can make from this study, then plan to follow up on that application next time.
7. Pray.

Other Resources:

- The Wheel (a Navigators resource found online) – draw it with the fellowship spoke way out of proportion, discussing that we tend to spend more time with other Christians than pursuing Christ through the other "spokes" (practices). Point out how bumpy a ride would be using these out-of-proportion wheels.
- Book 2, lesson 4, of the *Design for Discipleship* series from The Navigators
- Take mentee to church or a large-group fellowship event
- John 17
- 2 Corinthians 6:14–7:1 (marriage, dating, partnerships, etc.)

Relational Verses

Psalm 119:63 (NIV): *I am a friend to all who fear you, to all who follow your precepts.*

Proverbs 13:20 (NKJV): *He who walks with wise men will be wise, but the companion of fools will be destroyed.*

Proverbs 28:7 (NLT): *Young people who obey the law are wise; those with wild friends bring shame to their parents.*

Proverbs 28:24 (NIV) *Whoever robs their father or mother and says, "It's not wrong," is partner to one who destroys.*

1 Corinthians 15:33 (NIV): *Do not be misled: "Bad company corrupts good character."*

John 15:13 (NIV): *Greater love has no one than this: to lay down one's life for one's friends.*

Proverbs 12:15 (NIV): *The way of fools seems right to them, but the wise listen to advice.*

Proverbs 13:10 (WEB): *Pride only breeds quarrels, but wisdom is with people who take advice.*

Proverbs 19:20 (NIV): *Listen to advice and accept discipline, and at the end you will be counted among the wise.*

Proverbs 27:9 (NIV): *Perfume and incense bring joy to the heart, and the pleasantness of a friend springs from their heartfelt advice.*

Proverbs 4:14 (NIV): *Do not set foot on the path of the wicked or walk in the way of evil doers.*

Proverbs 24:1 (NIV): *Do not envy the wicked, do not desire their company;*

Luke 6:35 (NIV): *But love your enemies, do good to them, and lend to them without expecting to get anything back. Then your reward will be great, and you will be children of the Most High, because he is kind to the ungrateful and wicked.*

Proverbs 2:20 (NIV): *Thus you will walk in the ways of the good and keep to the paths of the righteous.*

Sample Lesson Plan
*Witnessing/The Gospel**

The "5 G's" may be used for two key areas: *assurance of salvation/the gospel* or *witnessing*. Go through the list itself with your mentee to make sure he or she understands the gospel and has become one of God's children or follow the lesson plan to teach your mentee how to use it with others.

Object: To equip my mentee with a tool that will help reach the world with the hope found through Christ.

Plan:
1. As always, begin with casual conversation, followed by prayer.
2. Write 5 G's in a vertical line down the page.
3. One at a time, finish writing each key word, verbally sharing the explanation. Take turns reading the accompanying verses with your mentee and ask him or her to share additional thoughts.
4. Ask your mentee whether he or she understands all the G's and their explanations.
5. Ask the mentee to learn and practice the tool for next time. Ideally, the "practice" will be sharing the gospel with someone by using the tool. At minimum, the mentee should practice it with a friend or family member.
6. Brainstorm a list of people who would benefit from hearing the 5 G's.

The 5 G's

GOOD – We are created *good* in God's image. We have inherent worth. This was Adam and Eve's situation. *Genesis 1:27, Ephesians 2:10*

GUILT – Sin separates us from God. We are guilty before Him. When Adam and Eve disobeyed God, they hid from God in their shame and guilt. *Genesis 3:8-11, Romans 3:23, 2 Corinthians 7:10*

GRACE – God couldn't stand being separated from us, so He sent Jesus to give us grace. *1 John 4:10, Ephesians 2:4-5, 8-9*

GOD'S PEOPLE – We become part of God's people when we receive this gift of grace. We are no longer alone. *John 1:12, 1 John 1:1-3*

GRATITUDE – This is what motivates us to live for God and in His grace. This is what motivates us to serve. Our obedience is a thank-you note to God. *Romans 12:1-2*

---

*Adapted from Dr. Kara E. Powell's seminar, "Sticky Faith: Practical Steps toward Building Long-term Faith in Young People," at the Christian Camp & Conference Center Association, October 23, 2014

Sample Lesson Plan
Meditation/Application
(Created from material taught by Debby Maschhoff)

This lesson will develop your and your mentee's understanding and practicing of Scripture meditation and application.

Objective: To help mentees understand how important meditation on and application of the Word are to our relationship with Jesus.

Plan:
1. Pray.
2. Communicate the following truths to the mentee:
   a. It's not just knowing the Word, but it's the life-changing aspect of it that counts (Psalm 1:1-2). It's the root system.
   b. There should be life-change when we're in the Word. The purpose of meditation is to become more like Christ (1 Peter 1:23–2:3).
   c. Mary modeled this as she pondered in her heart (Luke 2:19).
   d. Getting into the Word is not about the search or about the facts (though they can be fun). We're not supposed to fall in love with the Scripture itself. We need to fall in love with Whom it points us to: Jesus (John 5:39-40).
3. Have the mentee apply meditation through the "4 P's" exercise:

   Passage   What is God asking me to do or believe in this passage?
   Problem   How am I falling short?
   Plan   What can I do about it?
   Progress   How will I know when I've done it?

   Go through James 1:19-27 as an example. Then have the mentee do the 4 P's for a quiet time during the next week.
4) Pray.

Other Resources:
- Verse Analysis: A Meditation Study (included next)
- AEIOUs of Meditation (included next)
- The Word Hand (a Navigators resource found online)
- *Meditation* by Jim Downing

Verse Analysis
A Meditation Study
(Shared by Debby Maschhoff)

Use this easily adapted series of questions to go deeper in God's Word through analyzing a specific verse. Use it for your own study and share it with your mentees to help their growth.

1. Verse I am analyzing:

2. Pray for concentration, God's insights and an open heart.

3. Describe the context of the verse.

4. List one or more words from the verse, together with definitions.

5. List several cross-references to the verse.

6. Write the verse in your own words.

7. Visualize the setting or action and list any observations.

8. What application can you make of this verse?

AEIOUs of Meditation

This mnemonic device provides you and your mentees with simple steps to take when learning to practice scriptural meditation.

A – Ask questions (including word definitions)
E – Emphasize (a word, a phrase)
I – In your own words
O – Other verses (what else in Scripture relates to this?)
U – Use it! (or apply)

Reflect on what I am saying, for the Lord will give you insight into all this.
–2 Timothy 2:7 (NIV)

Walking by Faith with the Promises of God
By Tom Yeakley
The Navigators

This worksheet is a good exercise for introducing your mentee to claiming God's promises. Go deeper through reading Yeakley's book, Praying Over God's Promises.

How many folks estimate difficulties in the light of their own resources, and thus attempt little and often fail in the little they attempt. All God's giants have been weak men and women, who did great things for God because they counted on His faithfulness.

–Hudson Taylor

God's promises are never broken by leaning upon them.

–Howard Hendricks

I. ELEMENTS FOR ANSWERED PRAYER

In **Hebrews 6:12** the author writes, "We do not want you to become lazy, but to imitate those who through faith and patience inherit what has been promised." In the verse we find the three elements necessary to seeing God answer our prayers as we pray over the promises in His Word.

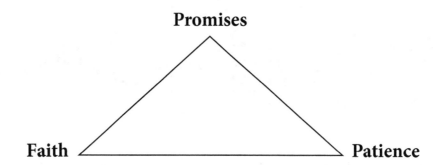

Promises

Faith   **Patience**

Triangle for Triumph

- Promises and Faith *without* Patience will lead to compromise and our trying to answer our own prayers.
- Promises and Patience *without* Faith will result in walking by sight, trusting in what is seen, and there will be a lack of dynamic in our lives.
- Faith and Patience *without* the Promises of God is presumption and can lead to great hardship and error.

II. FAITH

The promises alone, as great as they are, must be mixed with faith if we are to realize their fulfillment. The writer of Hebrews says, "Therefore, since the promise of entering his rest still stands, let us be careful that none of you be found to have fallen short of it. For we also have had the gospel preached to us, just as they did; but the message they heard was of no value to them, because those who heard did not combine it with faith" **(Hebrews 4:1-2)**. Certainly the writer is referring to the promise of salvation, but the principle is true that the promises of God must be combined with our faith for them to reach fulfillment.

What is Faith?

Faith is not a feeling or an impression. It is not that we convince ourselves of a truth, a kind of self-brainwashing. Faith is the simple acceptance and trust of a child; it is a trust that does not know possibilities or probabilities. It only sees the promise and the Promiser and expectantly hopes. It involves action, acting in accordance with what God has promised and fulfilling any conditions stated as necessary for God to fulfill His part of the promise.

2 Corinthians 1:8-11

1. God allows times of testing and trial; even for those seeking to live obedient, faithful lives.
2. God uses these difficult times to build faith and cause dependence on Him.
3. God has, will and will continue to deliver us from our difficulties as we trust Him.

Jeremiah 12:5   Exercise your faith "muscle"

Now, my beloved brothers and sisters, begin in a little way. At first, I was able to trust the Lord for ten dollars, then for a hundred dollars, then for a thousand dollars, then for one hundred thousand dollars, and now, with the greatest ease, I could trust Him for millions of dollars if there were occasion for it. But first, I should quietly, carefully, deliberately examine and see whether what I was trusting for was something in accordance with His promises in His written Word. If I found it was, the amount of difficulties would be no hindrance to my trust.

–George Mueller

III. PATIENCE

A. Waiting on God
Is God slow to answer? Why must we pray again and again?

Daniel 10:1-14
Matthew 7:7-11
Luke 11:5-8
Luke 18:1-8
Hebrews 10:36

- Prayer is not just asking, but communion.
- A mark of maturity is being able to enjoy the trip while you're on a detour.

B. Waiting and Action
How much are we to do while we wait? Do we only pray and wait?
Noah –   Hebrews 11:7
Abraham –   Hebrews 11:8
10 Lepers – Luke 17:11-19

God gives us the ground in answer to the prayer of faith, but not the harvest. That must be worked for in cooperation with Him. Faith must be followed up by works, prayer-works. Salvation is of grace, but it must be worked out if it is to become ours (Phil. 2:12).

And the prayer of faith is just the same. It is given to us by free grace, but it will never be ours until we follow it up, work it out. Faith and works must never be divorced, for indolence will reap no harvest in the spiritual world. I think the principle will be found to hold in any case where the prayer of faith is offered, but there is no doubt that it always holds good in cases where the strongholds of Satan are attacked, where the prey is to be wrested from the strong.

–J.O. Fraser

IV. ERRORS IN CLAIMING PROMISES

1. We can deceive ourselves (Jeremiah 17:9). Personal promises should stand the test of time and counsel. Because of the subjective nature in personal promises, we should always remember to use the other common means for determining the will of God:
    1. Word of God
    2. Personal Peace
    3. Godly Counsel
    4. Wise Thinking
    5. Open Doors of Opportunity

2. We sometimes believe that asking for ourselves is selfish. We fear that if we persist in our asking, then God will give us our desires to teach us a painful lesson. This is not the way our Heavenly Father treats His children.

    Psalm 106:14-15
    Psalm 78:17-31

    We are seeking to know and do God's will, not our own. We are not seeking to force God to act according to our will, nor are we demanding. We are simply asking.

3. We feel that if we ask with wrong motives, God will punish us. Our Heavenly Father always gives us what is best and good.

    James 4:3
    Matthew 7:9-11

Sample Lesson Plan
Faith and Obedience
(Created by Debby Maschhoff)

Faith and obedience are foundational character traits that should be taught early in the new or immature believer's journey. As stated in James 2:26 (NIV), "faith without deeds is dead." Faith and obedience are inseparable because faith is proven through obedience.

As an example of how lesson plans can be tailored to your own style, this sample lesson plan is in a slightly different format from the others.

Objective: To help the mentee see that Jesus is looking for people of faith who believe what He says in His Word.

Motivation: Read Hebrews 11 and discuss. Use example from your own life.
Key points to cover:
    1. Faith involves action.
    2. Faith is developed in hard situations.
    3. Faith has eyes on eternity.
    4. Faith involves a choice.
    5. Faith is willing to pay a price.
    6. Faith is in what God said.
    7. Faith is exercised between the time of promise and the time of fulfillment.

Plan:
    1. What is an area you are trusting God for?
    2. What does the Word say?
    3. Repeat for other areas.

Progress:
    1. Memorize verses on *practicing the presence of God* and on *the practice of faith*.
    2. Pray over situations in our lives.
    3. Give it to God in faith.

<h1 align="center">Sample Lesson Plan</h1>
<h2 align="center">Identity in Christ</h2>

This lesson plan on identity in Christ incorporates two very powerful resources: the "Fact-Faith-Feeling Train" and the "Who I am in Christ" handout by Freedom in Christ Ministries.[5] As with any lesson plan, you will need to adapt this according to your mentee's maturity as you proceed through the plan.

Objective: To help the mentee understand that his or her identity in Christ gives him or her inherent worth.

Plan:

1. Open with conversation and incorporate questions about how he or she finds his identity and worth. Examples: "How would you have described yourself in high school?" "When did you feel best about yourself growing up?" "What is the most important thing about you?" Share a little about your journey in this area, including how you believed lies versus truth about who you are, as well as how those choices affected you.

2. Pray.

3. Sketch a rough train, including an engine, one freight car and a caboose all linked together and on the move. Label the engine "Fact," the freight car "Faith," and the caboose "Feeling." Explain how it is the truth that needs to pull the train. People often try to let their feelings dictate how they live, but the caboose cannot effectively pull the train. That leads to trouble and ineffectiveness. We find the facts about who we are in God's Word.

4. Show him or her the "Who I am in Christ" list by Freedom in Christ Ministries. Go through it, asking questions about what stands out to him or her, what meets a need, etc. Ask his or her overall impression of these truths about him or her and how it affects him or her to read them. Are they hard to believe?

5. Discuss how, even if it is hard to believe at times, we need to choose truth over lies about the value God has given us. We need to put our *faith* in the *facts,* and the *feelings* will follow (pointing at appropriate train cars). Ask how he or she thinks believing these truths will affect his or her daily life and choices.

6. Ask what most stands out to him or her from this lesson. Make sure the mentee understands the train and the "Who I am in Christ" resources.

7. Ask how the mentee would like to apply this to his or her life. Determine a way you will provide accountability with this. Consider having him or her read the "Who I am in Christ" list daily until your next meeting.

8. Close in prayer, thanking God for these truths. If he or she is familiar with praying Scripture, you could pray through a section of "Who I am in Christ."

Other Resources:
- *Victory Over the Darkness* by Neil T. Anderson (adult version) or *Stomping Out the Darkness* by Neil T. Anderson and Dave Parks (teen version)
- "Self-image/Identity in Christ" Bible study (included next)
- *Rethink Your Self* by Trevin Wax
- *The Dream of You* by Jo Saxton
- *You Are Not Your Own* by Alan Noble.
- "Grace Gifts" handout[6]

Bible Study
*Self-image/Identity in Christ**

This Bible study may also be used for teaching identity in Christ.

1. Please list some things about yourself that you dislike, resent or would change if you could. Consider such things as your temperament, family, abilities, physical body, environment, etc.

2. For each of the following passages, answer each of the three questions:
   a. What is the truth?
   b. What should I do or not do?
   c. What should my attitude be?

   • Romans 8:28-29

   • Romans 12:3-6

   • Isaiah 45:5-10

   • Psalm 139:13-18

3. Return to what you wrote down for question 1. For at least two of the items you wish you could change about yourself, find the corresponding Scripture that speaks truth about that area of your life. Write down the lie you have been believing about that area of your life, followed by the truth you should believe. Cross out the lie. Example: My nose is too big is the lie I've believed. The truth is that God made me just the way I am, knitting me together in my mother's womb, knowing exactly what kind of nose He was giving me.

4. How are you going to apply what you have learned to your life? One possibility is learning the Scripture that cancels out the lie you have been believing. Each time the lie comes into your mind, remind yourself of the truth of that Scripture.

*Adapted from Doug Prensner's *Permanent Difference.*

Other Resources

Other resources mentioned throughout this book may be found by doing simple internet searches. For example, The Word Hand, The Prayer Hand, and the Topical Memory System (both the original and the "life issues" version) were all created by The Navigators and are readily available online. I also encourage looking up the pamphlet "7 Minutes with God: How to Plan a Daily Quiet Time" by Robert D. Foster. It can be purchased through Amazon or from other online retailers. Free versions are also available online.

Books that provide lessons for you to go through with your mentee include the following:
- *The 2:7 Series* by The Navigators
- *Begin: A Journey through Scriptures for Seekers and New Believers* by Ken Ham and Bodie Hodge
- *Growing in Christ: A 13-Week Course for New and Growing Christians* by The Navigators
- *Growing Together: Taking Mentoring Beyond Small Talk and Prayer Requests* by Melissa B. Kruger
- *Multiply: Disciples Making Disciples* by Francis Chan with Mark Beuving

Appendix B

How to Write a Lesson Plan

"Always include Jesus in your objective," Debby emphasized to me as she taught me how to write a lesson plan. "That will help ensure we are always focused on Christ."

That is good advice. After all, these mentoring relationships are about reaching the world for Christ. Even mundane (or exciting, depending on your personality) tasks such as writing a lesson plan are about helping others grow closer to Jesus.

As discussed earlier, you will want to accumulate good resources that you can use with your mentee. Writing a lesson plan will help you effectively use that resource. You also may create a lesson plan based on your personal study and knowledge of a specific subject.

As you write, remember that you will need your master copy of the plan and a separate worksheet for your mentee, along with copies of any supporting documents you will review together. This is similar to how teachers have an answer key to correspond with their student's homework papers.

Please keep in mind that not all mentors will use lesson plans. There are ways of being structural without following a lesson plan. Especially as you become more confident in your style and better understand your mentee, you will be able to determine how to best use your time together.

Steps for Writing Your Plan:

1. Pray and ask God for His guidance and help.
2. Determine the topic of the lesson. For this example, we will pretend you are creating a lesson from sermon notes about obedience.
3. Determine and write down the objective of the lesson, making sure to include Jesus. Example: "To help the mentee understand obedience as a reflection of our love for Christ and means of developing our intimacy with Him."
4. Write down the first steps of the lesson, which will involve some sort of conversation to reconnect and warm up, as well as opening in prayer. This conversation may incorporate discussion that leads up to your topic for the lesson.
5. Come up with an interesting way to engage your mentee with the material, if it does not already come up in your opening discussion. This may include sharing a story from your own life (either a personal story or something you have observed) or viewing/discussing something from pop culture or current events. Write down your plan for engaging your mentee as the next step in your lesson.
6. Transition into the sermon notes, either including them in the body of your lesson plan or having them readily available as an additional document. Go through the sermon notes, highlighting key points, asking good questions and reading relevant Scriptures together. This is the bulk of your lesson, and you can either detail it in one step or break down this portion into several steps.
7. Ask for highlights of what stood out to your mentee. Ask him or her, "What did you learn? What does it mean to you?"
8. Create a step for practical application. Ask your mentee how he or she will apply the material. Ask questions such as, "What are some ways it relates to you or others around you? How can you apply it?" Also consider using the GROW Acrostic in Appendix A to come up with ideas for application. Include a plan for accountability and/or follow-up.

9. Share any final thoughts on the lesson before closing in prayer.
10. Include a list of additional resources (for the same topic) at the bottom of your lesson plan. This allows you to figure out what you might study next with your mentee or provides further resources the mentee may use on his or her own. See the sample lesson plans in Appendix A for examples of how I do this.

The lesson plans you create will be useful not only for you as you lead your mentee, but also for your mentee as a resource he or she can use with others when he or she is ready to reach the next generation of mentees. For more helpful information, search "Hook Book Look Took" on the Internet. This method has enabled generations of Christ-followers to effectively teach the Bible to others.

Appendix C

Additional Notes for Mentoring High School Students

- When mentoring a high school student, it is crucial to understand that you are a mandated reporter. Please learn your state's guidelines and process for mandated reporting. Your primary concern is for your mentees, but it is important to know that you open yourself up to legal action if you do not follow the mandated reporter guidelines.
  - It would be wise for you to make a statement along these lines early in your mentoring relationship: "I want to develop trust with you, and I want you to know that I will keep our communication confidential. But I also need you to know that I have to follow the law, so there are certain things—like if you or someone connected to you is at risk—that I am required to share with others."

- Get to know your mentee's family, particularly the parents. You will be much more effective as a mentor if you have strong trust and open communication with the parents. This does not mean you serve as a pipeline for the parents' own agendas (e.g., "Please tell Terrell to clean his room!"), but it means you clearly state to your mentee's parents, "I realize what a privilege it is to influence your child. Please reach out to me at any time about concerns or to touch base. Our healthy communication is important."
  - As mentioned in the section about attitudes for mentoring, sometimes parents can feel threatened by mentors. After all, parenting teens can be incredibly difficult and a time when parents and children do not see eye to eye. The teen may be extolling your virtues at home while detailing the parent's failings. Please show empathy to the parents and let them know that you are ultimately working toward the same goal of helping the teen grow.
  - Here is a practical tip I give to mentors of teens: if you have permission to be in a car with your mentee, then do the work of walking to the door when you arrive to pick up the teen. The temptation is to simply text, "I'm here," but walking to the door allows you to interact with the person who answers it, whether that be a parent or sibling. These connecting opportunities develop into a greater, more effective ministry. Ultimately, you may become a blessing to the entire family.

- At the time of this writing, texting and social media are the primary means of communication for teenagers. It is helpful to know that many of them are averse to talking on the phone and that their social etiquette does not require responding to texts in a timely fashion. These are both areas of needed mentoring, but I do not recommend you address these things right away. These minor communication challenges are not your top priority, and you may immediately aggravate, cause stress or create a rift in your new relationship. Please do not take these generational behaviors personally.

- Try to not be offended if your mentee uses his or her phone during your meeting, especially at first. Seasoned mentor Maria Jun shares this anecdote:
  > I was mentoring a high school junior who used to look at her phone constantly and flip through Instagram and social media during our sessions. I was honestly a little offended

when this continued during the first three or four meetings. I felt like I was just pestering her while she would rather be doing something else, and that she didn't value our time together even though she showed up. I didn't want to force her to meet up and complained to my husband that maybe I shouldn't bother setting up another time to meet. We took a break during a holiday season, and, afterward, she really began to open up more. I realized that her phone was a defense mechanism she used when in new situations to deflect feeling awkward. She stopped doing that, and the relationship deepened.

- If you want to dig deeper, I have found that learning about generational characteristics is remarkably helpful in mentoring. My top source for this information is the Barna Group, which you can search online.

Appendix D

Helpful Books on Mentoring/Discipleship

The Complete Book of Discipleship: On Being and Making Followers of Christ by Bill Hull

Cultivate: Forming the Emerging Generation through Life-on-Life Mentoring by Jeff Myers, with Paul and Paige Gutacker

Down-to-Earth Discipling: Essential Principles to Guide Your Personal Ministry by Scott Morton

The Gentle Art of Discipling Women: Nurturing Authentic Faith in Ourselves and Others by Dana Yeakley

The Master Plan of Evangelism by Robert E. Coleman

Mentor for Life: Finding Purpose through Intentional Discipleship by Natasha Sistrunk Robinson

The Mentor Leader: Secrets to Building People and Teams That Win Consistently by Tony Dungy, with Nathan Whitaker

Organic Discipleship: Mentoring Others into Spiritual Maturity and Leadership by Dennis McCallum and Jessica Lowery

Endnotes

Foreword
1. Craig L. Blomberg and Darlene M. Seal, *From Pentecost to Patmos*, 2nd ed. (Nashville, Tennessee: B&H Publishing Group, 2021), 232.

Chapter One: The Impact of Mentorship
1. Howard Culbertson defines "creative access countries" as "countries where church activities are greatly restricted…where open evangelism by Christians is unlawful." Howard Culbertson, "Creative Access countries," Southern Nazarene University, accessed September 21, 2021, home.snu.edu/~hculbert/access.htm.

Chapter Two: Mentoring Basics 101
1. Culbertson, "Creative Access countries."

Chapter Three: Spiritual Multiplication
1. Kenny Burchard, "Greek-Geeking the Great Commission in Matthew," ThinkTheology.org, November 7, 2013, http://thinktheology.org/2013/11/07/greek-geeking-the-great-commission-in-matthew/.
2. Mark Moore, 2020 Online National Disciple-Making Forum, track session 3, April 29-30, 2020, https://discipleship.org/shop/digital-access-pass-online-2020-national-disciple-making-forum/.

Chapter Four: Three Aspects of Approach
1. To learn more about the Barnabas program, go to https://joyelgeneration.org/4-12-leadership-training/barnabas-program/.

Chapter Five: Three Essentials for Each One-to-One Meeting
1. Dirk C. Van Zuylen, "Discipling Like Jesus," *Discipleship Journal* (1999): 78.
2. Ele Parrott, *Transforming Together: Authentic Spiritual Mentoring* (Chicago: Moody Publishers, 2009), 57.
3. David Kinnaman and Aly Hawkins, *You Lost Me: Why Young Christians Are Leaving Church…and Rethinking Faith* (Ada, Michigan: Baker Books, 2016), 206.

Chapter Nine: The Best Way to Help Your Mentee
1. Robert E. Coleman, *The Master Plan of Evangelism* (Grand Rapids, Michigan: Revell, 2005), 79.
2. YouVersion (also known as Bible.com or the Bible App) is an online and mobile Bible platform published for Android, iOS, Windows Phone and many other operating systems; it also supports a variety of other platforms.
3. Operation World can be found at www.operationworld.org.
4. Scott Morton, *Down to Earth Discipling: Essential Principles to Guide Your Personal Ministry* (Colorado Springs, Colorado: NavPress, 2003), 127.
5. Ibid., 87.

Chapter Eleven: How to Find a Mentee
1. Jeff Myers, *Cultivate: Forming the Emerging Generation through Life-on-Life Mentoring* (Manitou Springs, Colorado: Passing the Baton International, Inc., 2010), 84.

Appendix A: Mentoring Resources and Sample Lessons
1. Kent Ira Goff, *The Soul of Tomorrow's Church* (Nashville, Tennessee: Upper Room Books, 2000).
2. Lance Witt, founder of Replenish Ministries. Witt's article with this quote is no longer available.
3. Goff, *The Soul of Tomorrow's Church*.
4. Ibid.

5. You can find the handout, "Who I am in Christ" by Freedom in Christ Ministries, at https://www.ficm.org/wp-content/uploads/2021/04/who-i-am-in-christ05.pdf.

6. You can find the handout, "Grace Gifts," at http://www.biblicalrestorationministries.org/depression_files/Grace%20Gifts.pdf.

Printed in the USA
CPSIA information can be obtained
at www.ICGtesting.com
CBHW060039160724
11412CB00020B/311